YORK NOTE

General Editors: Professor
of Stirling) & Professor Sul
University of Beirut)

Herman Melville

MOBY DICK

Notes by Wilson F. Engel

BA (OLD DOMINION UNIVERSITY) MA PH D (WISCONSIN)
Assistant Professor of English, Allentown College

LONGMAN
YORK PRESS

YORK PRESS
Immeuble Esseily, Place Riad Solh, Beirut.

LONGMAN GROUP LIMITED
Longman House, Burnt Mill,
Harlow, Essex CM20 2JE, England

First published 1981
Second impression 1985
ISBN 0 582 78177 9
Printed in Hong Kong by
Sing Cheong Printing Press Ltd

Contents

Part 1

Introduction

Life of the author

Born in New York City on 1 August 1819, to a family with Scottish and Dutch roots, Herman Melville received continuous formal schooling only until 1832. His father went bankrupt in 1830 and died in 1832. As a result, Herman Melville at the age of twelve began to maintain himself. He was successively a bank clerk, a farm hand, a store clerk, and a schoolmaster. For a short time he attended the Albany Classical School.

Melville's first sea voyage to Liverpool in England followed his futile attempt to become an engineer for the building of the Erie Canal. After his return from Liverpool, he tried school-teaching again, then travelled to Galena, Illinois, to work with an uncle, but could see no alternative to returning to sea. He shipped aboard the whaler *Acushnet*, bound for the Pacific Ocean, on 3 January 1841, and remained at sea until 14 October 1844.

Melville's first novels about his experiences on islands in the Pacific, *Typee* (1846) and *Omoo* (1847), were both popular and controversial. In 1847, through the editor Evert Duyckinck (1816-78), Melville became a regular contributor to New York magazines, and his style changed. In August 1847, Melville married Elizabeth Shaw, daughter of the Chief Justice of Massachusetts. His next novel, *Mardi* (1849), an allegory of the South Seas, was unpopular. Melville then wrote the romances *Redburn* (1849) and *White-Jacket* (1850) in haste to regain his popular readership.

In 1850 Melville purchased Arrowhead Farm in Pittsfield, Massachusetts; he struck up a stimulating friendship with the author Nathaniel Hawthorne (1804-64), who lived nearby; and he began *The Whale*, later renamed *Moby Dick*, which demonstrated his creative genius.

Moby Dick (1851) failed with both the critics and the public. Afterwards, Melville became increasingly reclusive, and his works became dominated by pessimism. His novel *Pierre* (1851) failed, and the stories that he wrote for *Putnam's Monthly Magazine* in the 1850s reflect Melville's increasing preoccupation with evil and human isolation. Even after a restorative voyage to England, Melville wrote

The Confidence Man (1857), a biting criticism of American commercialism.

Although 1857 marked the virtual end of Melville's career as a public writer, he began privately to publish poetry that is only today receiving the critical attention that it deserves: *Battle-Pieces and Aspects of the War* (1866), *John Marr, and Other Sailors; With Some Sea-Pieces* (1888), and *Timoleon* (1891). Left unfinished at Melville's death on 28 September 1891 was *Billy Budd, Sailor*, not published until 1924, now a classic of American literature.

The general historical background

Through westward expansion, political isolation from Europe and the American Civil War (1860-5), the United States became large, unified and powerful. Sixteen states in 1796, the United States contained forty-five in 1896. The frontier expanded from the Mississippi river to the Pacific Ocean, so that by 1893 Frederick Jackson Turner (1861-1932) could proclaim that there was no more frontier in America.

The centre for shipping and commerce during this period was New York City, and gradually during the century the centre of cultural influence shifted from Boston to New York. Immigration from Northern Europe continued throughout the nineteenth century and provided the labour for building railroads, canals, and roads. In the aftermath of economic depressions, such as the Panic of 1837, jobs were scarce for everyone, but northern manufacturing and commerce increased steadily.

The independent income of a political appointment was one possible means of obtaining support for a genteel way of living, but appointments were very difficult to obtain, even though the 'Spoils System' (the art of replacing former appointees with one's favourites) made the situation somewhat better than it had been before Andrew Jackson's presidency (1828-36). People capable of management in general were turned away. Under a veneer of democracy, the United States was becoming a land of rich, powerful families and common labourers, bound together through commercialism.

The literary background

Publishing out of New York, Washington Irving (1783-1859) and James Fenimore Cooper (1789-1851) captured wide audiences with their romances. In New England Ralph Waldo Emerson (1803-82) preached that the world is charged with meaning and that man can fulfil himself by understanding the basic goodness in himself and in

Nature. Edgar Allen Poe (1809-49) and Nathaniel Hawthorne (1804-64) revealed the evils within the human mind. Melville disliked the writings of Irving and Cooper, and *Moby Dick* steers a middle course between the idealism of Emerson and the pessimism of Poe and Hawthorne.

Relevant ideas

America, having declared independence from England in 1776, began almost immediately to seek a unique national identity through literature. A sophisticated literary image of America was finally achieved in Melville's writings and in those of Walt Whitman (1819-92).

Melville's writings all show the influence of the ideas of John Calvin (1509-64), who emphasised (*i*) the sinfulness of all men, (*ii*) the predestined salvation or damnation of men from the creation of the world, (*iii*) the very small number of those chosen to be saved for the rewards of heaven, and (*iv*) the justification of the chosen ones, whereby God lets them know their future salvation while they live.

Several of Melville's characters are noble savages. By Melville's time it was fashionable to idealise the primitive people of the world for their natural simplicity and for their gift of living in harmony with a rationally ordered and benign Nature.

Fedallah, the Parsee in *Moby Dick*, is a Zoroastrian from India, the follower of a religious sect originating in Iran in the seventh century BC. Zoroastrians consider the sun and fire to be symbols of the Almighty, and believe that in a cosmic struggle between the gods of good and evil, the good will win. Zoroastrians are prone to fatalism, the belief that they can do nothing about the events to come.

A note on the text

Melville's manuscript of *Moby Dick* is no longer thought to be extant. The first American edition of the novel, published by Harper and Brothers, New York, 1851, and the first English edition, published by Richard Bentley, London, 1851, are the bases for all later responsible editions. Since Melville himself was responsible for some of the divergences between these editions, the two must be considered together. Melville included some notes to his text, usually included in modern editions. For a list of good modern editions, see the 'Suggestions for further reading' on pages 92-4.

Part 2

Summaries
of MOBY DICK

A general summary

Ishmael, the narrator of the story, with his cannibal friend Queequeg, ships aboard the *Pequod*, a whaler from Nantucket, bound for the Pacific Ocean. Ahab, captain of the whaler, is a one-legged man with acute intelligence and with a maniacal obsession to revenge himself on the great white whale called Moby Dick, who bit off his leg. Ishmael, fascinated with the whale trade, gives a detailed account of the whaling operations aboard the *Pequod* and often digresses from his narrative of Ahab's progressive madness to explore all aspects of whale classification, anatomy, natural history, legends and uses.

Ahab, at first reclusive, declares his quest for Moby Dick to the crew and offers a gold doubloon, nailed to the mast, to the first man who sights the hated whale. The *Pequod* searches the Atlantic whale grounds, taking whales as they are sighted. The ship continues round the Cape of Good Hope, through the Indian Ocean and the South China Sea, and finally into the Pacific Ocean without any certain sighting of Moby Dick. Other whalers are sighted along the way, some with tales of Moby Dick, and they provide a contrast to the *Pequod*. The white whale is at last sighted in the Japanese Cruising Ground.

Recognising Ahab's unhealthy obsession, Starbuck, the first mate of the *Pequod*, has tried throughout the voyage to dissuade his captain from following the whale. He even considered shooting Ahab, but faltered. Evidence of Ahab's obsession abounds. Ahab's special precautions for killing the whale include the diabolical fabrication of a special harpoon, the barbs tempered with the blood of his three pagan harpooners, a special boat crew, and Fedallah, a Parsee skilled in telling fortunes from signs.

The chase of the white whale is heralded by portents. Nature seems to tell Ahab to turn away. But Ahab confronts the whale three times. On the last try, caught in the lines of harpoons stuck on the whale's back, Ahab is pulled to his death. The whale, apparently enraged by the *Pequod's* insistent pursuit, batters the ship with his head and sinks it, then departs. The only survivor of the wreck is Ishmael, who is kept afloat by Queequeg's coffin-turned-lifebuoy and rescued by the *Rachel,* whose captain is searching for a son last seen pursuing Moby Dick.

Detailed summaries

Introductory matter

The inscription: *Moby Dick* is inscribed to Nathaniel Hawthorne (1804-64), the American novelist whose brooding preoccupation with human evil fascinated Melville; he made Hawthorne's acquaintance and visited him frequently during the writing of *Moby Dick*.

The etymology *(Supplied by a Late Consumptive Usher to a Grammar School):* gives the etymology of the word *whale,* and the word for *whale* in thirteen languages.

Extracts *(Supplied by a Sub-Sub-Librarian):* seventy-nine passages from biblical, literary, and historical works are quoted as a panoramic view of whales and whaling in the imagination of man.

Chapter 1. Loomings

Ishmael, the narrator, claims to have no money and to be bored by life on the land. He has decided to go whaling because he longs to sail on the mysterious ocean. He supposes that this whaling voyage forms part of the 'grand programme of Providence'.

NOTES AND GLOSSARY:

Ishmael:	in the Bible, Ishmael, the son of Abraham and Hagar, sent into the wilderness with his mother because of the jealousy of Abraham's wife Sarah. See Genesis 21:14
hypos:	morbid depressions of spirits
Cato:	the Roman Cato the Younger (95-46BC), who committed suicide after bidding his followers make peace with his enemy Caesar
Manhattoes:	inhabitants of Manhattan Island
mole:	breakwater
spiles:	piles
Saco:	Saco river, which runs to the Atlantic in southern Maine
Niagara:	the famous Niagara Falls, extending between New York and Canada
Rockaway Beach:	on Long Island
brother of Jove:	Poseidon, god of the sea, in Greek mythology
Narcissus:	a figure in classical mythology whose self-love led to his destruction

salt:	experienced sailor
river horse:	hippopotamus, literal translation of the Greek word
Van Rensselaers:	an upper-class family of New York
Randolphs:	an aristocratic family of Virginia
Hardicanute:	Harthacanute, King of Denmark (1035-42), and of England (1040-2)
Seneca:	Lucius Annaeus Seneca (3BC-AD65), the Roman stoic
Stoics:	disciples of the school of philosophy, founded by Zeno of Citium in the fourth century BC, which stressed the virtues of forbearance, endurance, and fortitude
hunks:	a crusty, old person
money . . . the root of all earthly ills:	almost a direct quotation from the Bible, 1 Timothy 6:10
on no account . . . heaven:	a paraphrase from the Bible, Matthew 19:24
Pythagorean maxim:	Pythagoras (582-507BC), the Greek philosopher, forbade the eating of beans because they caused flatulence
Providence:	a theological term for God's foreknowledge of all human history
conceits:	ideas

Chapter II. The Carpet-Bag

Ishmael travels to New Bedford and arrives on a Saturday night in December, too late to catch the shuttle boat to Nantucket. Unable to afford good lodgings, Ishmael proceeds towards the waterfront where the very cheapest inns are. He stumbles into a Negro church service by mistake and fancies himself among black angels of hell. Farther on he decides to enter the Spouter-Inn.

NOTES AND GLOSSARY:

packet:	packet-boat or mail-boat
Tyre of this Carthage:	Phoenicians from Tyre in Syria founded Carthage
bowsprit:	spar projecting ahead of ship to which jib sails are attached
grapnels:	four-pronged anchors used for dragging
Gomorrah:	the wicked biblical city destroyed with Sodom according to Genesis 19:24
Tophet:	a place near Jerusalem, Tophet became synonymous with hell

pea coffee:	chick-pea coffee
Euroclydon:	a classical storm from the east or north-east
Paul's tossed craft:	St Paul was shipwrecked on Malta according to the Bible, Acts 27:14
old black-letter:	an early printed book
Lazarus:	the neglected beggar in the Bible, who entered heaven according to Luke 16:19-25
Dives:	the rich man who neglected Lazarus and went to hell according to Luke 16:19-25
Orion:	an equatorial constellation resembling the Greek mythological Boeotian giant
Sumatra:	a large island of the Dutch East Indies, west of the Malay Peninsula
Moluccas:	the Spice Islands between Celebes and New Guinea in the Dutch East Indies
Czar in an ice palace:	an ice palace was constructed annually in St Petersburg
temperance society:	a society which preached abstinence from drinking all intoxicating beverages

---

Chapter III. The Spouter-Inn

The old landlord 'Jonah' tells Ishmael that he must sleep in a bed with a dark-complexioned harpooner. Reluctantly Ishmael resolves to go to bed in the harpooner's room, only to be awakened by a huge man entering with an embalmed head in his hand. The man, tattooed all over his body, takes an idol from his bag, worships it, and springs into bed with a tomahawk pipe between his teeth. Ishmael's fearful cries bring the landlord Peter Coffin (called 'Jonah'), who introduces Queequeg the cannibal as Ishmael's bed partner. Ishmael resigns himself to fate and sleeps soundly.

NOTES AND GLOSSARY:

bulwarks:	ship's side above deck level
New England hags:	the Salem 'witches' of the 1690s
squitchy:	squishy or very wet (the only example of the use of the word in the *Oxford English Dictionary*)
four primal elements:	earth, air, fire, and water
Hyperborean:	far-northern
Cape of Blanco:	there are too many Capo Blancos to guess which is meant
Jonah:	the unfaithful prophet who was swallowed by a whale according to the Bible, Jonah 1:17
his poison:	slang for alcoholic beverage
goggling glasses:	glasses bulging inwards to limit the capacity

gulph down:	gulp down
Skrimshander:	a name for a sailor, from the activity of carving in whalebone, known as scrimshaw work or scrimshandering
monkey jacket:	short, close-fitting jacket worn by sailors
green box coat:	loose overcoat
sartainty:	certainty
the Feegees:	Fiji
comforters:	long woollen scarves worn round the throat as protection from the cold
brimmers:	cups filled to the brim
coffer-dam:	watertight structure fixed to a ship's side so that repairs can be made to the ship below the waterline
brown study:	melancholy, thoughtful, or pensive mood
green:	inexperienced
done brown:	chastened thoroughly
Mt Hecla:	Mount Hekla, an active volcano in Iceland which erupted in 1845
'balmed:	embalmed
inions:	onions
turning flukes:	doing a whale's dive, or going to bed
spliced:	slang for married
vum:	vow
land of Nod:	sleep
Thirty Years' War:	general European war, fought 1618-48
sabbee:	savvy or understand

Chapter IV. The Counterpane

Ishmael, awakening at daybreak, feels caught in the hug of the sleeping cannibal, Queequeg. He shakes Queequeg awake and watches him dress and bathe. Out of delicacy, the cannibal pulls on his hat and boots while under the bed; then, emerging from under the bed, he pulls on his trousers, washes and shaves with the razor-sharp edge of his harpoon.

NOTES AND GLOSSARY:

counterpane:	coverlet, or quilt
Cretan labyrinth:	mythological maze built on Crete to house the Minotaur, the bull-man monster
Newfoundland dog:	large dog, first known in Newfoundland and whose origin was unknown in Melville's time
staving about:	rushing or dashing about

Chapter V. Breakfast

Ishmael expects a lively conversation at the breakfast table; instead all the whalemen are quiet, and Queequeg, seated at the head of the table, coolly reaches over everyone to grab rare beefsteaks. After eating, Queequeg smokes in the public room while Ishmael takes a walk.

NOTES AND GLOSSARY:

satin wood:	a smooth, golden-brown wood
Ledyard:	John Ledyard (1751-89) who travelled to the Pacific Islands, Russia, and Siberia
Mungo Park:	Park (1771-1806) was an explorer who travelled in Africa
Green Mountains:	in Vermont, USA

Chapter VI. The Street

Walking around New Bedford, Ishmael muses on the curious foreigners to be encountered in the major seaports of the world. But for him New Bedford is superior to the others because of the cannibals and savages there. Strange and comical to Ishmael are the green inlanders of Vermont and New Hampshire, who have left the farm for whale fishing. The city is wealthy from the success of the whaling industry. Whaling money has provided fine houses, gardens, and rich dowries.

NOTES AND GLOSSARY:

Regent Street:	the well-known street of shops in London
Broadway:	a famous street in New York
Chestnut:	a street in Philadelphia
Apollo Green:	in Bombay
Water Street:	in Liverpool
Wapping:	an area in London
unholy flesh:	because they are pagans and because they have eaten men
Feegeeans . . . Brighggians:	natives from the islands of Fiji, Tonga-tabu, Erromanga, Pannangia, and Brighggia, the last probably fictitious
sou'wester:	waterproofed hat with a neck flap
bombazine cloak:	coat of twilled dress-material
straps:	braces or suspenders *(American)*
Canaan:	the biblical land of milk and honey, according to Exodus 3:8
scoria:	waste or dross from the smelting process
Herr Alexander:	a German magician, contemporary of Melville

Chapter VII. The Chapel

On a second stroll Ishmael visits the Whaleman's Chapel, which is full
of sailors, sailors' wives, and widows. To Ishmael's surprise,
Queequeg is in the congregation. Ishmael contemplates both the grief
of those who have lost loved ones at sea and human mortality in
general.

NOTES AND GLOSSARY:

Off-shore Ground: south-west of the Galapagos Islands in the Pacific
Ocean

cave of Elephanta: small island in Bombay harbour, noted for its
ancient temples, carved out of solid rock caves

Goodwin Sands: treacherous sands off north and east Kent, in
England, where many ships were wrecked

Adam . . . sixty round centuries ago: in the nineteenth century the
earth was thought to be around six thousand years
old, as in the Bible

stove boat: bashed-in boat

brevet: temporary promotion

Jove: Jupiter, chief of the gods in classical mythology

Chapter VIII. The Pulpit

Father Mapple, the ex-sailor and ex-harpooner who has dedicated his
life to the ministry, enters, covered with ice and melting sleet from the
storm. The pulpit is fitted with a ladder like the perpendicular side-
ladders used in mounting a ship from a boat at sea. After mounting
the pulpit, Father Mapple draws the ladder up, isolating himself. The
pulpit's front is like a whaling vessel, and the Bible rests on what looks
like a ship's figurehead. Ishmael concludes that 'the world's a ship on
its passage out, and not a voyage complete; and the pulpit is its prow'.

NOTES AND GLOSSARY:

headed: finished

little Quebec: the Canadian city which is naturally fortified by a
bluff three hundred feet high

Ehrenbreitstein: village with fortress overlooking the Rhine

where Nelson fell: on his flagship at the Battle of Trafalgar (1805)

fiddle-headed beak: wood, carved like a violin's head as a figurehead

Chapter IX. The Sermon

Father Mapple's sermon is a moralised and modernised version of the
biblical story of Jonah and the whale. He tells the story twice. In the

first telling, he emphasises Jonah's repentance for his attempted flight from God's commands. Jonah pays for his passage from Tarshish to Joppa; the ship on which he sails is beset by storms; the crew cast Jonah overboard when they discover that he is the cause of the storm; Jonah is swallowed by the whale and patiently endures God's just punishment. The swinging lamp in Jonah's cabin, in this version, is a symbol of Jonah's conscience.

In the second telling, Father Mapple emphasises Jonah's mission as pilot and prophet, and he prophesies woe to the preacher who, like Jonah, is a castaway. Father Mapple's peroration promises delight to the man who 'ever stands forth his own inexorable self' and takes God as his only law and lord.

NOTES AND GLOSSARY:

larboard:	left side, facing the prow, of a ship, now called *port*
starboard:	right side, facing the prow, of a ship
midships:	gather in the centre of the ship
hymn:	Psalm 18, as adapted from the version used in the Dutch Reformed Church
'And God . . . Jonah':	in the Bible, Jonah 1:17; throughout the sermon Father Mapple introduces quotations from Jonah alongside his own version of the words spoken by the biblical characters
son of Amittai:	Jonah
evil eye:	a reference to the widespread belief that the glance of certain people can have harmful effects
spile:	pile
steel tags:	on leather trappings
shroud:	line from the masthead to some lower point
shoots to . . . teeth:	quickly closes together its jaws
ground swell:	swell or heavy rolling of the sea caused by a distant storm or earthquake
Pilot Paul . . . castaway:	in the Bible St Paul is a castaway, 1 Corinthians 9:27
top-gallant:	highest sail on a mast

Chapter X. A Bosom Friend

At the Spouter-Inn Queequeg is carving the nose of his wooden idol. The cannibal then takes up a book and counts the pages. Ishmael discerns in Queequeg 'the traces of a simple honest heart'. He gradually grows to love the cannibal and explains what he can to him about the book. Ishmael proposes that they smoke together as a token of friendship; then Queequeg grasps him and says that they are married. Going to their room, Queequeg invites Ishmael to worship with him the Negro idol. Ishmael joins his new bosom friend in his devotions. The two then sleep, 'a cosy, loving pair'.

NOTES AND GLOSSARY:

phrenologically: according to the study of character through the shape of the skull

General Washington: George Washington (1732-99), first President of the United States

Socratic wisdom: knowledge of the self

Presbyterian Church: direct heir of Calvinism, the teachings of John Calvin (1509-64)

Chapter XI. Nightgown

After short naps, Ishmael and Queequeg awaken at midnight and smoke together. In the blue haze of the pipe smoke, Queequeg tells about his native island and history.

NOTES AND GLOSSARY:

nappishness: sleepiness (the only example of the use of the word in the *Oxford English Dictionary*)

Chapter XII. Biographical

Queequeg's Story: Queequeg is a native of Kokovoko, an uncharted island. His father is a High Chief or King; his uncle is a High Priest; he is descended from brave warriors. Because he thinks that he can learn from Christians 'the arts whereby to make his own people happier than they were; and more than that, still better than they were', from childhood he desires to see Christendom. So he leaps aboard a Sag Harbour whaler as it departs his island and is turned into a whaleman. But not only do Christians seem wicked, they also convince Queequeg that the whole world is wicked and that he should die a pagan. In fact, Queequeg feels that he has been so tainted by his contact with evil Christians that he cannot return to his native throne until he feels himself 'baptised again'.

Ishmael and Queequeg plan to ship aboard the same whaler.

NOTES AND GLOSSARY:

Sag Harbour: on Long Island, one of the great nineteenth-century whaling ports

Czar Peter: Peter the Great of Russia (1672-1725), who himself laboured in the British Royal Naval Yard to gain the technological expertise to start a Russian navy.

Chapter XIII. Wheelbarrow

Ishmael and Queequeg, on Monday morning, check out of the Spouter-Inn and, with their belongings stowed in a borrowed wheelbarrow, proceed to the *Moss,* the little sailing vessel that runs to Nantucket. Aboard, Queequeg turns over in the air a man who has mimicked him. The man complains to the captain of this, but just as the captain is rebuking Queequeg, the man is struck overboard by the escaped boom. Queequeg calmly leaps into the sea and saves him.

NOTES AND GLOSSARY:

block:	a barber's block, a wooden head for a wig
Rokovoko:	Kokovoko
calabash:	gourd used for drinking
Tartar air:	savage air
lubber:	lover, here land-lover or land-lubber
bevy:	very
weather sheet:	line to windward controlling the boom
boom:	swinging horizontal spar attached near the bottom of the schooner's main sail
joint-stock:	common-fund, in which each person has a share

Chapter XIV. Nantucket

Ishmael tells the traditional American Indian story of Nantucket's discovery: the island is found when Indian parents seek their infant, who has been carried off by an eagle. From that time, the Nantucketers have roamed the oceans of the world freely.

NOTES AND GLOSSARY:

Eddystone lighthouse:	a lighthouse on dangerous rocks off the coast of Cornwall, England
Laplander:	from Lapland in northern Europe
quohogs:	derived from the Naraganset Indian name for common round clams
Bhering's Straits:	Bering Strait
Himmalehan:	like the Himalayan mountains
Alexanders:	resembling the Macedonian Alexander the Great (356-323BC)
three private powers:	Russia, Austria and Prussia divided Poland among them in the late eighteenth century
Texas:	annexed to the United States in 1845
Cuba upon Canada:	the United States seriously considered expansion into these areas in the nineteenth century
chamois:	European wild antelope

Chapter XV. Chowder

Ishmael and Queequeg lodge at the Try Pots. Mrs Hosea Hussey, wife of the owner, serves the two men excellent chowder, the only meal available any time at the Try Pots. Mrs Hussey allows no harpoons in her rooms since young Stiggs, having come home from a luckless voyage of four and a half years, committed suicide with his.

NOTES AND GLOSSARY:

Try Pots: besides the name of the inn, pots for 'trying' oil from blubber

opened . . . larboard: saw to the left

made a corner three points to the starboard: come to a corner that was about 33 degrees measured from dead ahead to the right

Chapter XVI. The Ship

Queequeg tells Ishmael that Yojo, his idol, has insisted that Ishmael proceed alone to select the whaling vessel and to ship for himself, irrespective of Queequeg. Since the following day is one of fasting and devotion for Queequeg, Ishmael proceeds to ship aboard the venerable old whaler the *Pequod,* named for a now-extinct tribe of Massachusetts Indians. Her old chief-mate Peleg, now one of her owners, had decorated the *Pequod* with whalebone so that her bulwarks seem a single gigantic jaw and her tiller is carved from the lower jaw of a whale.

Inside a wigwam, whose supports are of whalebone, Ishmael finds Captain Peleg. Ominously Peleg speaks of the ship's Captain Ahab, whose leg has been eaten off by 'the monstrousest parmacetty that ever chipped a boat'. Ishmael says he wants to go whaling so as to see the world, and Peleg sends him to look out on the ocean, implying that the vision of open ocean is all he is liable to see on his voyage. Still firm in his decision, Ishmael is taken below to meet Captain Bildad, another owner of the vessel. Bildad assents to shipping Ishmael aboard, and Peleg begins the process of signing him on. Expecting the '275th part of the clear nett proceeds of the voyage', Ishmael is surprised when Peleg finally signs him for the 300th part. After signing, Ishmael tells the owners about Queequeg, whom they wish to see.

Ishmael leaves the ship, but he returns when he realises that he has not seen Captain Ahab. Peleg reminds Ishmael that he is already shipped and tells him that Ahab is shut up in his house. Ishmael has doubts about the biblical name Ahab, owned by the king whose blood dogs licked. Peleg says that the name Ahab was given him by his crazy widowed mother, who died when he was one year old. An old squaw, Tistig of Gayhead, has said his name would prove prophetic. Peleg gives his personal testimony that Ahab is 'a swearing good man', though moody and sometimes savage since he lost his leg. Ahab has a wife and child too: 'Ahab has his humanities!' Ishmael departs with feelings of awe and pity for Ahab.

NOTES AND GLOSSARY:

XXXIX Articles: essential doctrine of the Church of England

Tit-bit: besides the name of a ship, a delicacy

Medes: inhabitants of Media, overthrown by Cyrus around 842BC

luggers: vessels with a square or lug sail

butter-box galliots: Dutch light-draft vessels

claw-footed look: like old furniture fitted out with ball and claw feet

like a French grenadier's . . . Siberia: like that of a veteran of Napoleon's Egyptian and Russian campaigns

three old kings of Cologne: bones of the Magi who visited the new-born Christ were preserved in the Cathedral of Cologne

Becket: Thomas à Becket, Archbishop of Canterbury, murdered in 1170

Thorkill-Hake: Thorkill Hakr, hero of Icelandic sagas

Tartar: savage Asian tribesman

Pottowottamie Sachem's head: Algonquin chief's scalp

pins: belaying pins, wooden pegs placed in racks, to which lines may be tied

sheaves: the moving wheel of a pulley

parmacetty: sperm whale

lungs: voice

weather-bow: windward bow

transom: transverse beams attached to the sternpost of a ship

chancery wards: persons whose guardians are the courts

timber head: top end of a timber, rising above the gunwale and serving for belaying lines

Quaker: member of the Society of Friends, a Christian religion to which Peleg, Bildad, and Ahab belong

conscientious scruples: the conscience was equated with the Holy Spirit by the Quakers, who refused to fight men

tuns: casks holding about two hundred and fifty gallons

shad-bellied: nickname for Quakerish; sloping gradually from the front to the tails

boat-header: mate who steers the boat and kills the whale after it has been harpooned

Categut whaleman:	one from the Kattegat Straits between the Baltic and North Seas
marlingspike:	marlinespike, a pointed metal tool used to separate the strands of rope in splicing
dost:	Ishmael's confusion makes him use the familiar second-person singular form for *do*
ship's articles:	contract
stiver:	Dutch coin of little value
'Lay not up . . .':	from the Bible, Matthew 6:19-21
drawing:	displacing
Ahab of old:	the biblical Ahab of 1 Kings 16:30 and 21:19
Gayhead:	or Gay Head, western tip of Martha's Vineyard in New England

Chapter XVII. The Ramadan

Convinced that his friend's ritual must be over, Ishmael goes to Queequeg's room. Although he knocks and calls and peers through the keyhole, no answer from Queequeg is forthcoming. Ishmael guesses that Queequeg has had a fit, and he breaks open the door to find Queequeg sitting on the floor in a trance with his idol on his head. He will not move, so Ishmael goes to sleep. At daybreak Queequeg breaks his trance and professes his friendship for Ishmael. Concerned on account of his friend's religious fanaticism, Ishmael decides to reason with him. But Ishmael's train of thought leads to a discussion of indigestion, which in turn inspires Queequeg to tell of an incident of cannibalism. Ishmael concludes that his missionary efforts are futile. The two proceed to the *Pequod*.

NOTES AND GLOSSARY:
pilau: Oriental dish with rice, meat, spices, and raisins

Chapter XVIII. His Mark

The very sight of Queequeg brings protestations from Captain Peleg, who did not expect Ishmael's friend to be a cannibal. Bildad joining him, the two captains insist that Queequeg prove that he is a Christian. Hard-pressed, Ishmael pleads that Queequeg is a member of the all-encompassing worshippers of the world. Peleg is mightily impressed with Ishmael's rhetoric and asks whether the cannibal has ever struck a fish. As a reply, Queequeg flings his harpoon over Bildad's head directly into a small pool of tar he has indicated. Amazed at this display of accuracy, Peleg calls for the papers to sign Queequeg on at the generous wages of a ninetieth part.

NOTES AND GLOSSARY:

Quohog:	common round clam, here Peleg's blunder for Queequeg
Belial:	a servant of the Devil
Bell . . . dragon:	in the apocryphal 'Bel and the Dragon' Daniel triumphed over superstitions
afterclaps:	unexpected events after an affair is supposed to be over
Davy Jones':	the sailors' Devil or spirit of the sea
jury-masts:	makeshift masts
top sail:	sail directly above the lowest sail of a mast
waist:	between the forecastle and the quarterdeck

Chapter XIX. The Prophet

Just after Ishmael and Queequeg leave the *Pequod,* a shabbily dressed man with a pock-marked face accosts them with portentous hints about Captain Ahab. He asks whether the two have seen 'Old Thunder', as Captain Ahab is called, and the two admit that they know very little about him. So the man, known as Elijah, tells them the dockside lore about Ahab and hints vaguely about the doomed voyage that is about to take place.

NOTES AND GLOSSARY:

confluent small-pox: with the scars all run together

skrimmage:	skirmish
Elijah:	biblical prophet in the reign of Ahab, according to 1 Kings 21:19-23

Chapter XX. All Astir

The *Pequod* is being readied for sea, with provisions for three years. Captain Peleg sits in his wigwam watching the hands, and Captain Bildad does the purchasing and providing of stores. Bildad's sister, 'Aunt Charity', fetches extras for everyone. Ishmael and Queequeg often visit the ship in hope of seeing Ahab, but in vain. Ishmael remains unsatisfied that he must sail without a glimpse of him.

NOTES AND GLOSSARY:

costermongers: fruiterers

Chapter XXI. Going Aboard

Early on Christmas day, Ishmael and Queequeg go to the *Pequod* because they know she will be sailing. In the mist they see sailors running ahead towards the ship. From behind, Elijah clasps both on their shoulders and asks them whether they can find the sailors whom they just saw. He mumbles a strange warning; then he says he shall see them soon at the Last Judgement. On the *Pequod* the sailors are nowhere in sight. Finally they arrive, but Ahab remains in his cabin.

NOTES AND GLOSSARY:

Grand Jury: Last Judgement
scuttle: hatchway with a lid
perry dood: very good

Chapter XXII. Merry Christmas

Captains Bildad and Peleg muster the crew. As they get underway Ishmael is kicked by Peleg for his slackness and finds Peleg a virtual bundle of energy inspiring his crew to work. At twilight the ship is at sea and Bildad and Peleg reluctantly depart in their sail-boat, leaving the ship on its own.

NOTES AND GLOSSARY:

under weigh: with the anchor raised from the bottom
marquee: large tent
handspikes: bars for heaving about the windlass
stave: stanza
Booble Alley: depraved neighbourhood in Liverpool, or any such place
Watts: Isaac Watts (1674-1748), hymn writer
'Sweet fields . . . between': from a hymn by Isaac Watts
offing: the region some distance off the shore
both stormy Capes: Cape Horn and the Cape of Good Hope
main-yard: yard on the mainmast on which the mainsail is extended
tierce: one-third of a pipe, or about forty-two gallons

Chapter XXIII. The Lee Shore

The helmsman of the *Pequod* is the same Bulkington who was introduced in Chapter III. He has just landed after a dangerous four-year voyage and shipped aboard the *Pequod* immediately. For Ishmael, Bulkington is a symbol of courage, a kind of demi-god who does the best that man can, even to his death.

NOTES AND GLOSSARY:

Some chapters back: Chapter III
crowds all sail off shore: sets all sails to reach the open sea
apotheosis: transformation into a god

Chapter XXIV. The Advocate

Ishmael defends the reputation of whaling men. Whaling men are butchers, but this form of butchery is far superior to that of the battlefield. All the oil lamps of the world burn to the glory of whaling men. But whaling men have historically been honoured, and their business brings in millions of dollars. Whale ships have been pioneers of discovery, of trading routes, and of missionary activity. The whaler's literary heritage extends back to the Book of Job in the Bible. In England the whale is a royal fish. One Roman general included a whale's bones in his triumph. The constellation Cetus raises whaling to heavenly heights. Besides, for Ishmael, whaling is an education equal to the best to be had.

NOTES AND GLOSSARY:

tapers:	waxed wicks, used to light candles
De Witt's time:	Jan de Witt (1625-72), the Dutch statesman; at one time the Dutch were one of the great whaling people
Louis XVI of France:	the victim (1774-93) of the French Revolution
that Egyptian mother:	possibly the Nile river
Cook or Vancouver:	Captain James Cook (1728-79) and George Vancouver (1758-98), great explorers
Cookes:	men like Captain James Cook
your Krusensterns:	Adam Johann von Krusenstern (1770-1846), a Russian who circumnavigated the globe
discovery . . . Dutchman:	the Dutch were the first to land on Australia, in 1606
Polynesia:	the central Pacific Islands, south of Hawaii
Job:	the Leviathan is described in the Bible, Job 41
Alfred the Great:	an English king (871-99) who wrote an Old English version of Orosius's *Historia adversus Paganos,* in which he placed the account of whaling
Edmund Burke:	Irish statesman and philosopher (1729-97) who spoke in favour of America before the American Revolution
Benjamin Franklin:	Franklin (1706-90) was an American printer, scientist, and statesman
triumphs . . . Roman general:	Marcus Aemilius Scarus (first century BC)
Cetus . . . South:	in the southern hemisphere
great captain of antiquity:	not certainly identified
small but high hushed world:	heaven

Chapter XXV. Postscript

Ishmael adds that whale oil is used at British coronations to symbolise the sacred acquisition of kingship.

NOTES AND GLOSSARY:
saltcellar: container for salt at the table
quoggy: quaggy, or soft

Chapter XXVI. Knights and Squires

Starbuck, a Nantucketer and a Quaker, is the Chief Mate on the *Pequod*. He is thin and wiry, a man of actions, not words. He is inclined to superstition, but of a kind that springs from intelligence, not ignorance. He often thinks of his wife and child, and he places a high value on his boatmen's fear of whales. He is courageous, but not to the point of foolhardiness. His father and brother perished in the whaling trade. In ordinary peril, Starbuck is a tried man; in the face of unusual spiritual terror, he is probably vulnerable.

NOTES AND GLOSSARY:
patent chronometer: clock designed to compensate for the ship's movements
Bunyan: John Bunyan (1628-88), author of *The Pilgrim's Progress*
Cervantes   (1547-1616): author of *Don Quixote,* who lost his arm at the battle of Lepanto
Andrew Jackson (1767-1845): a great American President from humble back-woods origin
kingly commons: Ishmael celebrates the noble dignity of the common man

Chapter XXVII. Knights and Squires II

Stubb, the second mate, is from Cape Cod. Easy-going and careless, he is calm in his duties, even in the jaws of danger. He is not an inquisitive or intelligent man, even about divine things. Flask, the second mate, is from Tisbury in Martha's Vineyard. Choleric, short, and somewhat foolhardy, he follows the whale for fun. He is nick-named 'King-Post' because of his steadiness of aim. Queequeg is Starbuck's harpooner; Tashtego, an Indian from Gay Head, is Stubb's harpooner; Daggoo, a coal-black Negro slave, is Flask's harpooner. The rest of the crew are from all over the world. All these men follow Ahab to their deaths.

NOTES AND GLOSSARY:

rigadig imitative of the sound of the tunes (the only example of the use of the word in the *Oxford English Dictionary*)

wrought nails and cut nails: forged or cut with a die

headsmen: men in command of a whaling boat; see 'boat-header' in the notes to Chapter XVI

Prince of the Powers of the Air: the Devil, named in the Bible, Ephesians 2:2

Ahasuerus: Hebrew form of Xerxes in the Bible

ring bolts: iron bolts with rings at their heads

halyards: lines for hoisting or lowering sails

before the mast: quarters for non-officers; the phrase is by extension applied to crew members

Anacharsis Clootz: Jean Baptiste Clootz (1755-94) theatrically led a group of foreigners before the French National Assembly in 1790 to demonstrate the sympathy of all mankind with the French Revolution

Chapter XXVIII. Ahab

As the ship runs southwards, the weather warms up, but before the winter weather is left behind, Ahab first appears on his quarter-deck. He stands like a hero of old with a ghastly white mark running down his face and neck into his clothes. According to an old Gay-Head Indian aboard, this mark first appeared when Ahab was forty years old from 'an elemental strife at sea'. Ahab's ivory peg leg is stuck in one of two auger holes cut for the purpose in the deck. Ahab seems resolute, fearless, and dedicated, a king in silence and bearing. Every day thereafter, Ahab appears.

NOTES AND GLOSSARY:

taffrail: rail around the ship's stern

quarter-deck: part of upper deck, between poop and mainmast

Cellini's cast Perseus: a bronze statue of Perseus holding up the snaky-locked head of the slain Medusa, by Benvenuto Cellini (1506-71)

Manxman: from the Isle of Man in the Irish Sea

mizen shrouds: lines for the mizzen mast

Chapter XXIX. Enter Ahab; to Him, Stubb

Pacing the deck, Ahab makes a noise with his ivory leg that threatens the crew's sleep. Stubb hints that he could wrap his ivory leg with tow so as to muffle its noise, but Ahab takes offence. Stubb, insulted and wondering at his captain's words, fancies that Ahab may have kicked him.

NOTES AND GLOSSARY:

Quito:	Ecuadorian city so high in the Andes mountains that is has temperate weather, even though it is near the Equator
griping:	grasping
globe of tow:	ball of prepared hemp
wad:	ram in a wad as if into a cannon barrel
filling one:	filling a shroud or death robe; Ahab puns on the other meaning of shroud-rope
Dough-Boy:	besides the name, a boiled, flour dumpling
Tic-Dolly-row:	*tic douloureux (French),* twitching of the face
worse nor:	worse than

Chapter XXX. The Pipe

Like an enthroned potentate, Ahab sits on an ivory stool and smokes. But the pipe gives him no pleasure, so he hurls it overboard.

NOTES AND GLOSSARY:

Khan:	title given to the successors of Genghis Khan, supreme ruler over Turkish, Tartar, and Mongol tribes and Emperor of China in the Middle Ages

Chapter XXXI. Queen Mab

The next morning Stubb tells Flask that he has dreamed that Ahab kicked him with his ivory leg. When Stubb kicked back, he kicked his right leg off. Then Ahab seemed to be a pyramid, and Stubb kept kicking it and stubbing his toe. A merman rebuked Stubb for his kicks and offered his posterior instead. But the merman's flanks were covered with marlinespikes, so Stubb forbore. Just as Stubb was about to resume kicking the pyramid, the merman reasoned that, since Ahab's initial kick was delivered with an ivory leg, there could be no ill will; to the contrary, the kick was an honour. Stubb concludes that the best policy is to let the captain alone.

NOTES AND GLOSSARY:

Queen Mab:	Queen of the Faeries in sixteenth-century English literature, but also the dream-bringer in Shakespeare's *Romeo and Juliet*
Slid:	an oath, 'God's lid'

chimney hag:	witch in the chimney corner
garter-knights:	Knights of the Order of the Garter
mast-head:	lookout on the topgallant crosstrees

Chapter XXXII. Cetology

Ishmael offers three main categories for whales by size—folio, octavo, and duodecimo. Like these book sizes, whales are proportionally the same, though in different lengths. Under folio whales, the first presented is the sperm whale, 'the largest inhabitant of the globe'. Under octavo whales, the black fish, Ishmael maintains that 'Blackness is the rule among almost all whales'.

NOTES AND GLOSSARY:

fain:	gladly
Charing Cross:	in London, where royal proclamations were publicly read
tauntings in Job:	in the Bible, Job 41:1-11
binocular heart:	heart with two compartments
penem intrantem feminam mammis lactantem: (Latin)	'a penis entering the female that suckles with teats'
ex lege naturae jure meritoque: (Latin)	'on account of the law of nature justly and deservedly'
folio:	book whose size is that of one sheet folded once
octavo:	book whose size is that of one sheet folded three times
duodecimo:	book with twelve pages printed per sheet
packet-tracks:	major mail routes
gnomon-like:	like the gnomon, the column that casts the shadow on the sundial
Ahaz-dial:	from the Bible, Isaiah 38:8
Cain:	according to the Bible, Genesis 4:14-15: 'the Lord set a mark upon Cain, lest any finding him should kill him'
Mephistophelean:	diabolical or devilish
tallow:	animal fat
folder:	paper-knife
hartshorn:	literally deer's horn; ammonia
Black Letter:	here *Principal Navigations* (1598) by Richard Hakluyt (?1552-1616)
Queen Bess:	Queen Elizabeth I (1558-1603) of England
Feegee fish:	fish with the proverbial fierceness of a Fiji Islander
bright waist:	white paint around hull halfway between the waterline and the rail

mere sounds . . . signifying nothing:	alludes to Shakespeare's *Macbeth* V, 5, 26-8: 'a tale/Told by an idiot, full of sound and fury,/Signifying nothing'
draught:	draft

Chapter XXXIII. The Specksynder

Ishmael gives the history of the position of harpooner. Formerly command of a whaler was divided between the captain and an officer called the 'specksynder', who was Chief Harpooner, responsible for all whaling activities aboard. Although now he ranks below even the captain's officers, his importance on a voyage is great. Socially he is equal to the men before the mast; professionally he is well above them.

NOTES AND GLOSSARY:

Mesopotamian:	from Mesopotamia, thought to be the site of the earliest civilisation
imperial purple:	Roman emperors were privileged to wear this colour on their togas
in terrorem:	*(Latin)* 'to inspire terror'
princes of the Empire:	princes of the Holy Roman Empire
hustings:	election campaigns

Chapter XXXIV. The Cabin-Table

At the cabin-table Ahab commands the meal with an awesome bearing. None dares speak, and a strict decorum is observed. After the officers have eaten, the harpooners Queequeg, Tashtego, and Daggoo eat. Their meal is eaten savagely, and Dough-Boy, the steward, is terrorised by them.

NOTES AND GLOSSARY:

Emir:	Turkish title of honour
binnacle:	the case in which the compass is kept
main brace:	a rope reeved through a block at the end of a yard to control its angle, here on the mainmast
hornpipe:	a lively sailor's dance
Grand Turk's head:	head of the Sultan of Turkey
Abjectus:	*(Latin)* castaway
Belshazzar:	more magnificent than fortunate, according to the Bible, Daniel 5
Coronation Banquet at Frankfort:	held after the election of the Holy Roman Emperor
hearse-plumed:	horses in funeral processions wore black plumes

carlines:	carlings, pieces of timber running fore-and-aft between two of the transverse beams supporting the deck
wild Logan:	James Logan (?1725-80), an Indian chief named after a Scotsman. His family was massacred by whites and he sought revenge

Chapter XXXV. The Mast-Head

From the first day at sea to the last, the mast-head watches are set so that whales may be sighted. The history of mast-head watches on land and on sea is traced by Ishmael from the ancient Egyptians to the present day, including all the world's pedestalled statuary.

NOTES AND GLOSSARY:

skysail poles:	uppermost part of a mast, above where the skysails are set
truck:	small wooden block with holes for halyards at the top of a mast
Saint Stylites:	Saint Simeon Stylites (fifth century) lived thirty-five years upon a small platform on a pillar
Napoleon:	Napoleon Bonaparte (1769-1824), Emperor of France
Louis Blanc:	French politician and journalist (1811-82)
Louis Philippe:	King of France 1830-48 (1773-1850)
Louis the Devil:	Louis Napoleon Bonaparte, President of France, 1848-52, later Emperor
Great Washington:	George Washington (1732-99), the first American President
Admiral Nelson:	Horatio, Lord Nelson (1758-1805), English naval hero
Obed Macy:	author of *The History of Nantucket* (1835)
Colossus of old Rhodes:	one of the Seven Wonders of the World, a bronze statue of the sun god Helios in the harbour of Rhodes
case-bottle:	flask shaped to fit in a case
Phaedon instead of Bowditch:	Plato's *Phaedo* instead of Nathaniel Bowditch's *New American Practical Navigator* (1802). See note on Bowditch in summary to Chapter 99
Platonist:	idealist
Childe Harold:	hero of Byron's poem *Childe Harold,* from which the verses 'Roll on . . . vain' are taken (Canto IV, Stanza 179); Melville has substituted 'blubber hunters' for 'fleets'

Cranmer's . . .ashes: a confusion of the martyr Thomas Cranmer, burned in 1556, and the fourteenth-century reformer William Wycliffe, whose ashes were cast in a brook in 1428

Descartian vortices: René Descartes (1596-1656) postulated that the world is comprised of innumerable spiritual vortices

Pantheists: those who believe that God is in everything

Chapter XXXVI. The Quarter-Deck

Near evening Ahab orders all hands aft. He hammers a Spanish ounce of gold, the reward for sighting the white-headed whale, to the mast. Then he announces his intention to pursue Moby Dick to the death, and his crew are heartily in favour of the pursuit. Moved by their acceptance of this quest, Ahab must still explain himself to the incredulous Starbuck, who sees no sense in gaining revenge on a brute. Ahab explains that the brute surface of the whale for him represents or symbolises an 'inscrutable malice' that he must kill. Starbuck gains some intellectual apprehension of Ahab's design and by the force of Ahab's rhetoric is reduced to acquiescence. Gathering his crew about the capstan, Ahab looks into each man's eye to assure his assent. He then grasps the crossed harpoons of his harpooners and eyes his three officers, who turn their faces. He makes all swear death to Moby Dick as drinks are served by his sworn pagan harpooners.

NOTES AND GLOSSARY:

sixteen dollar piece: worth of a doubloon
top-maul: hammer
tarpaulins: caps of canvas, waterproofed with tar
twisketee betwisk: twisted
split jib: ripped triangular stay-sail stretching from the outer end of the jib-boom to the foremast head
razeed: reduced the number of decks of a ship; here, ate off the leg of
Norway Maelstrom: the Moskenstrom
tawn: tan
St Vitus's imp: who leads people in a wearying, perplexing course
Pope washers . . . beggars: ceremony performed on the Thursday before Easter
seizings: cords attaching metal heads to the harpoon shafts
ratifying sun: the approving sun, which waits to pass judgement on the matter

Chapter XXXVII. Sunset

Ahab is surprised that all his crew submitted to his will, and he admits to Starbuck's accusations that he is mad. In the imagery of iron rails, he expresses his indomitable purpose to track and kill the whale.

NOTES AND GLOSSARY:
This is the first chapter in which Ishmael is not visibly the narrator of the events.

Iron Crown of Lombardy: used in the coronation of the Holy Roman Emperor

Burkes . . . Bendigoes: Jim Burke and William 'Bendigo' Thompson were English prize fighters of the 1830s and 1840s

long gun: long rifle

Chapter XXXVIII. Dusk

Starbuck marvels that his will has been subordinated to that of a madman. He considers the present array of the ship to be like a division of life itself: forward is the drunken crew; aft is the brooding silence of the mad captain. In between these forces Starbuck sees the horror that life is a moment of knowledgeable submission, an awareness of the impelling forces and of their inexorable consequences.

NOTES AND GLOSSARY:
demigorgon: Demogorgon, a mysterious god of the underworld

Chapter XXXIX. First Night-Watch

Stubb laughs about the strange events of the day. Claiming all things to be predestined, he finds laughter to be the best reaction to the apparent absurdity of recent events.

NOTES AND GLOSSARY:
Like Chapter XXIX, this chapter is introduced with dramatic form. Throughout the book narration gives way to drama.

Stubb solus: *(Latin,* as in a stage direction) Stubb alone

brace: rope attached to the yard for trimming the sail

Mogul: Mongol ruler

'We'll drink . . . meeting': from the song 'Sparkling and Bright' by Charles Fenno Hoffman (1806-84) of New York

Chapter XL. Midnight, Forecastle

The crew sing and dance, and only a few allusions are made to Ahab's quest. A storm blows up and contentions arise. Then Daggoo and the Spanish sailor fight. But the storm is very strong, and all men scatter to save the ship. Little black Pip, who has been asked to dance and play the tambourine during the change of the watch, asks God for mercy in the face of Ahab's mad determination.

NOTES AND GLOSSARY:

forecastle:	short raised deck at the fore-end of the ship
foresail:	the principal sail on the foremast
'Farewell . . . commanded':	from the song 'Spanish Ladies'
'Our Captain . . . whale':	from the song 'Captain Bunker' and two other sea songs, 'The Mermaid' and 'The Bonny Ship the Diamond'
Eight bells:	twelve o'clock midnight
Mogul's:	of a Mongol ruler
Star-bo-leens:	starbolines, the starboard watch, which alternates with the port watch
ground-tier butts:	bottom barrels in the lowest storage hold
copper-pump:	liquid-transfer pump
Indian file:	in a line, each person stepping in the tracks of the one in front
double-shuffle:	kind of dance
windlass-bitts:	upright posts supporting the windlass
pagoda:	an eastern temple, often hung with bells
Lascar:	from Lashkar, India
Brahma:	the creator, first member of the Hindu trinity
douse sail:	lower sail quickly
Seeva:	Siva, the destroyer, third member of the Hindu trinity
chassee:	kind of dance
Heeva-Heeva:	Tahitian dance
reefing:	reducing the extent of a sail
Cattegat:	Kattegat, a channel between the North and Baltic Seas
St Jago's Sailor:	from Sao Tiago *(Portuguese)*, one of the Cape Verde Islands
arrah:	really
White squalls:	squalls of great violence
jib-stay:	rope from the fore-topmast to the jib sail
royal yard:	supports the fourth level of sails above the deck
anaconda:	South American boa; a snake

Chapter XLI. Moby Dick

The tales of the White Whale have spread for years and now form a continuous whole. Moby Dick is thought of as ubiquitous since he appears in different places at the same time. He is also thought to be immortal because he is seemingly indestructible. Unusual for his whiteness and for his deformed lower jaw, the whale is also malevolent, seeming to delight in human destruction. In a scene of shattered boats and ravaged men, Ahab struggled to kill this whale with a knife, only to lose his own leg in the whale's jaws. While suffering in madness over the pain in his body and the malignity of the whale, Ahab 'came to identify with him, not only all his bodily woes, but all his intellectual and spiritual exasperations'. Ahab has become a monomaniac, intent on killing the whale, which he now sees as a symbol of all the evil in the world.

NOTES AND GLOSSARY:
Ishmael is again clearly the narrator for the first time since Chapter XXXV.

I, Ishmael: compare with the opening of Chapter I
Olassen and Povelson: authors of *Travels in Iceland* (1805)
Cuvier's: of Baron Georges Cuvier (1769-1832), the French naturalist
Nor'West Passage: way through the Arctic Seas from the Atlantic to the Pacific
Strello mountain: Serra da Estrêla, highest mountain range in Portugal
Arethusa fountain: in Greek mythology the nymph Arethusa, transformed into a fountain, escaped by flowing under the sea to Syracuse in Sicily
Arkansas duellist: frontier brawler
No turbaned Turk . . . malice: alludes to Othello's words just before his suicide in Shakespeare's *Othello* (V)
Ophites: from *ophis* (Greek: serpent), a group of Gnostic sects opposed by early Christian writers
Patagonian Cape: Cape Horn
Hotel de Cluny: in Paris
stun' sails: studding sails, set on detachable extensions of yardarms in calm weather to catch more wind
Thermes: from *thermae* (Latin: hot baths). These are beneath the Hôtel de Cluny
Caryatid: supporting column carved like a human figure
Job's whale: Leviathan, in the Bible, Job 41
a seventy-four: warship with seventy-four guns

Chapter XLII. The Whiteness of the Whale

White is the colour of Moby Dick. Though a symbol of purity and nobility, nevertheless, white in itself is appalling, even causing terror in its very name. Ishmael sees white as a symbol of something men fear but cannot understand; white is 'the most meaning symbol of spiritual things'.

NOTES AND GLOSSARY:

japonicas: ornamental plants originating in Japan

Pegu: kingdom of Lower Burma that flourished from the sixth to the eighteenth century

Hanoverian: of Hanover, a state in Germany

overlooking Rome: the Holy Roman Empire

white stone . . . joyful day: commonplace in ancient Roman lyric poetry of white stone for a good and black stone for a bad day

wampum: shell beads used as money or for other purposes, some symbolic

Persian fire worshippers: Zoroastrians; see Part I of these notes

Jove . . . a snow-white bull: in this form Jove abducted Europa and took her to Crete

Passion of our Lord: celebrated the last week in Lent

Vision of St John: in the Bible, the Book of the Revelation of St John the Divine

heraldic coat: coat of arms

Coleridge: Samuel Taylor Coleridge (1772-1834), author of *The Rime of the Ancient Mariner*

Xerxes: fifth-century Persian king

bluff-bowed: forthright

White Squall: squall of great violence

Froissart: Sir John Froissart (*c.*1333-*c.*1405), author of *Chronicles of England, France and Spain,* translated by Lord Berners, Part I, Chapter 350

pallid horse: Death's horse in the Bible, Revelation 6:8

Whitsuntide: seventh Sunday after Easter, Pentecost, commemorating the descent of the Holy Spirit

White friar . . . White Nun: Carmelite and Cistercian

White Tower of London: oldest building in the Tower of London complex

White Sea: in northern Russia

Yellow Sea: between China and Korea

Blocksburg: scene of the Witches' Sabbath in the Harz mountains in central Germany

Pizzaro:	Francisco Pizzaro (*d*.1541), conqueror of Peru
snow-howdahed Andes:	mountains that seem to have snow-white elephant saddles on them
white-lead:	for making paint
hypo:	morbid depressions of spirits

Chapter XLIII. Hark!

After midnight as men are passing buckets of water hand to hand to fill the scuttle-butt, Archy whispers to Cabaco, a Cholo Indian, that he hears a cough below, signifying the presence aboard of someone not yet seen above decks. Archy claims that a word of such has passed between Stubb and Flask.

NOTES AND GLOSSARY:

middle-watch:	on from midnight to four in the morning
scuttle-butt:	drinking vat
Cholo:	half-breed Peruvian Indian
Caramba!:	*(Spanish)* exclamation of surprise

Chapter XLIV. The Chart

Ahab ponders charts and old log books to plot the most likely route along which to find Moby Dick. Deliberately he has sailed early in the year so that, instead of making for the waters off Japan immediately around Cape Horn, he may leisurely hunt for the whale on a course around the Cape of Good Hope. He plans to reach the Japanese waters at just that time one year from the day of sailing when Moby Dick is liable to be present. Ahab's single-minded quest gives him vivid dreams and moments of frenzied anxiety, as if his unquiet soul and patient mind are at war.

NOTES AND GLOSSARY:

tithe:	tenth
Mufti:	expounder of Mohammedan law
Prometheus:	Greek mythological figure, punished by Zeus for taking fire to men; he was chained to a rock, where a vulture or eagle feasted on his liver

Chapter XLV. The Affidavit

Ishmael documents instances when sperm whales were struck but escaped and finally were slain. Then he lists the names of four whales so well known for their fierceness that they have legendary significance among the whalemen. That fishing for whales is perilous he proves by citing the high mortality rate on whaling voyages. The power of sperm whales is coupled with a seemingly conscious malevolence. In numerous instances whales have turned on ships and sunk or damaged them, as if in revenge.

NOTES AND GLOSSARY:
Some examples from this chapter are from Melville's own history. Most of the time Ishmael is clearly a narrator who is clearly not Melville; in this chapter Ishmael's voice and Melville's voice become confused; Ishmael is here almost Melville.

Rinaldo Rinaldini: probably Rinaldo the fierce hero of medieval romance

Cambyses King of Persia in the sixth century BC

Timor: Timor Sea, between Timor and Australia

Ombay: Alor, north of Timor across the Ombai Strait

Marius or Sylla: rivals during the first great civil war of Rome (second century BC)

Captain Butler: Lieutenant-Colonel William Butler, hunter of Indians

Annawon: captured by Captain Benjamin Church during King Philip's War

Indian King Philip: leader (d.1676) in the Indian war of New England

Moses . . . plagues of Egypt: the biblical story is told in Exodus 7-12

Owen Chase: author of *Narrative of the . . . Shipwreck of the Whale-Ship Essex, of Nantucket* (1821)

Saul . . . fright: the biblical story is told in Acts 9:3-4 and 6

Langsdorff's Voyages: George Heinrich von Langsdorff (1774-1852), author of *Voyages and Travels*

Captain D'Wolf . . . nephew: John De Wolf married the sister of Melville's father

Lionel Wafer: author of *A New Voyage* (1699)

Dampier: William Dampier (1652-1715), author of *Voyage Round the World* (1697)

Juan Fernandes: Chilean islands in the South Pacific

Solomon . . . sun: From the Bible, Ecclesiastes 1:9

Barbary Coast: comprising Tripolitania, Tunisia, Algeria, Cyrenaica, and Morocco

brit: the food of the right whale. For a full description, see Chapter LVIII

Chapter XLVI. Surmises

Ahab sees usefulness in keeping his men at work doing their trade. By allowing the taking of other whales than Moby Dick, Ahab can provide the crew with the oil for cash earnings and the owners with healthy profits.

NOTES AND GLOSSARY:
perspective: prospective

Chapter XLVII. The Mat-maker

Tashtego cries from aloft, 'There she blows!'. A whole school of whales blow and dive, tails in the air. Ahab calls for the exact time. All preparations are made to pursue the whales, but just then the crew realise that around Ahab are five dark figures not seen before above the deck.

NOTES AND GLOSSARY:

sword-mat:	matting used to protect parts of the rigging
lee-beam:	side of the ship away from the wind
fluke:	horizontal tail of the whale
line tubs:	housings for the harpoon lines
samphire:	aromatic plant whose leaves are used in the making of pickles
gunwale:	side of the whaleboat

Chapter XLVIII. The First Lowering

The five shadowy figures, one of whom, Fedallah, seems a devil, stand by Ahab's own boat. Four boats are lowered, including Ahab's. As the boats close with the whales, a squall whips up. But Queequeg is already in the bow and thrusts home, just as the storm strikes. In the dawn, still in a storm, Starbuck's crew abandon their boat just in time as the *Pequod* rams and sinks her in the poor visibility.

NOTES AND GLOSSARY:

Manillas:	Philippine Islands
gudgeons:	little fish
steel-bits:	cutting edges
marling-spikes:	marlinespikes, metal tools tapered at one end for use in splicing rope
seethe her:	make the water seem to boil around her
hintings of . . . Elijah:	in Chapter XIX
peaked:	with oars raised vertically, set in holes adjacent to the oarsmen
three seas off:	three waves away
rack:	broken clouds
waif pole:	used to mark the position of a dead whale

Chapter XLIX. The Hyena

When brought aboard the *Pequod,* Ishmael meditates about the absurdity of the recently stove boat, and he proceeds to make out his will.

NOTES AND GLOSSARY:

oil-jacket:	jacket waterproofed with linseed oil
Lazarus:	a man raised from the dead by Christ; see the Bible, John 11

Chapter L. Ahab's Boat and Crew. Fedallah

Ahab's special boat and devilish crew would certainly be a surprise to the *Pequod's* owners, but after the initial shock of their presence, the crew are no longer disturbed by them—except by Fedallah, a mystery to the last.

NOTES AND GLOSSARY:

plug-hole:	drain hole
Tamerlane's:	of Tamburlaine, the fourteenth-century Mongol conqueror
thole pins:	these are fixed in pairs on the boat's rails to serve as oarlocks
Beelzebub:	Old Testament pagan god, New Testament devil
according to Genesis:	In the Bible, Genesis 6:2 and 4
Rabbins:	Jewish theologians who wrote around the time of Jesus Christ

Chapter LI. The Spirit-Spout

Off south-west Africa Fedallah sights a ghostly whale spout. Days later and thereafter with the same frequency the solitary jet appears. Rumour spreads that the jet is Moby Dick's and that the whale is luring the ship into remote seas to turn and wreck her.

NOTES AND GLOSSARY:

trump of judgement:	the Last Judgement, as described in the Bible, in Revelation
taffrail-breeze:	from astern
stays:	ropes supporting the masts
Cape Tormentoto:	Cape Tormentoso, according to Bartholomew Diaz, who rounded it in 1486
bowlines:	knots to form loops in the ends of a rope
tell-tale:	remote cabin compass

Chapter LII. The Albatross

After four years of whaling the *Goney* (Albatross) is rusty and her men are in rags. When Ahab calls over for news of Moby Dick, the captain of the *Goney* drops his megaphone into the sea, an ominous sign. The small fish that formerly followed the *Pequod* now follow the *Goney*.

NOTES AND GLOSSARY:

tyro: tiro, or novice
fullers: those who cleanse and thicken cloth
in the wind: with sails catching the wind on their fronts
Up helm: turn upwind
Cyclades: in the Aegean Sea
Islands of King Solomon: either the Solomon Islands in the South Pacific or the Old Testament seaport Ophir, source of Solomon's wealth

Chapter LIII. The Gam

A gam is 'a social meeting of two (or more) whale ships, generally on a cruising-ground, when, after exchanging hails, they exchange visits by boats' crews: the two captains remaining, for the time, on board of one ship, and the two chief mates on the other'. A gam was a normal occurrence when two ships met. That Ahab 'would not after all, perhaps, have boarded' the *Goney* is significant.

NOTES AND GLOSSARY:

Fanning . . . King's Mills: islands in the central Pacific Ocean
ducking of ensigns: rendering honours by dipping ensigns
Dr Johnson: Samuel Johnson (1709-84), author of *Dictionary of the English Language* (1755)
Noah Webster's ark: Webster's *American Dictionary of the English Language* (1828)
after-oar: farthest oar to the stern

Chapter LIV. The Town-Ho's Story

In a gam with the *Town-Ho,* the crew learn of the story of the Laker Steelkilt and the Nantucketer Radney, whose mutual hatred ended in Radney's death in the jaws of Moby Dick and in Steelkilt's flight to Tahiti. Curious is the untold secret that Steelkilt whispers to the captain, so powerful as to stop him from flogging or pursuing Steelkilt.

NOTES AND GLOSSARY:

hull hove out:	tipped on its side
Callao:	major Peruvian port, near Lima on the Pacific coast
Mackinaw:	Fort Mackinac in the Straits of Mackinac between Lake Huron and Lake Michigan
peltry:	covered with pelts
Winnebago:	Wisconsin Indians
Borean:	northern
Bowie-knives:	broad-bladed knives, named after Jim Bowie, the American frontiersman
sheeted-home:	stretched out to their limits.
scupper-holes:	drain holes
Charlemagne:	in AD800 crowned Emperor of the West; also a hero of romance
cannikin:	small drinking-vessel
billeted at:	officially assigned to
backstays:	ropes from the upper mast-heads to both sides of the ship to help support the masts
chicha:	fermented liquor made from maize by natives of South America
Mohawk counties:	in central New York State
Ashantee:	ferocious tribe native of West Africa
Inquisition:	Spanish Inquisition to search out heresy from 1478 to 1820
Sydney men:	men from Australia
whale-pike:	for pushing whale-blubber about the decks
Turn to:	get to work
mincing knives:	long knives with handles at both ends for cutting blubber in very thin strips
handspikes:	wooden bars used as levers
companion-way:	stairway
try-pots:	vessels in which blubber is 'tried' into oil
ship's run:	part of a ship's bottom that rises from the keel and narrows toward the stern
Teneriffe:	largest of the Canary Islands
main-chains:	assemblage that extends the basis of the shrouds of the mainmast outside the ship's side
bowsman:	oarsman who sits nearest to the bow
heaving down:	tipping over
poop:	raised stern deck
Holy Evangelists:	the four Gospels, used here to mean the Bible
Auto-da-Fés:	public burnings of those condemned by the Inquisition as heretics

Chapter LV. Of the Monstrous Pictures of Whales

From the earliest Indian representations to the most recent engravings, artists have been mistaken in their renderings of the whale. But Ishmael admits that there is no way to find out exactly what a whale looks like.

NOTES AND GLOSSARY:

Saladin: Saladin (1137-93), the great Moslem warrior

St George: the patron saint of England, who is usually depicted in full armour

cavern-pagoda of Elephanta: on the island in Bombay Harbour

Matse Avatar: incarnation of Vishnu, the second god of the Hindu trinity, in the form of a fish

Guido: Guido Reni (1575-1642)

Hogarth: William Hogarth (1697-1764), English painter and engraver

howdah: seat for riding on an elephant

Sibbald: Sir Robert Sibbald, a seventeenth-century Scottish naturalist and physician

jets d'eau: *(French)* springs of water

Saratoga: resort in New York State

Baden-Baden: resort in Germany

Advancement of Learning: by Francis Bacon (1561-1626), English philosopher and statesman

hippogriff: fabulous creature, like a griffin, only with a body of a horse

Richard III whales: hump-backed, as Richard III is portrayed in Shakespeare's *Richard III*

Platonian Leviathan: the ideal form of a whale

Jeremy Bentham's skeleton: Jeremy Bentham (1748-1832), English utilitarian philosopher, willed his skeleton to the University of London, where it is displayed in his usual clothing

Chapter LVI. Of the Less Erroneous Pictures of Whales, and the True Pictures of Whaling Scenes

Of the four published outlines of the sperm whale, Ishmael considers Beale's to be the best. The Frenchman Garneray has done the best action scenes involving whaling.

NOTES AND GLOSSARY:

Garnery: Ambroise-Louis Garneray (1783-1857), French painter

cutting-in: removing blubber from the whale
hove over to: as if moored to

Chapter LVII. Of Whales in Paint; in Teeth; in Wood; in Sheet-Iron; in Stone; in Mountains; in Stars

---

Ishmael leaves speaking of high art and turns to popular art and the art of nature herself for representations of the whale.

NOTES AND GLOSSARY:
kedger: cadger, beggar
busks: braces for corsets
skrimshander: sailors' whalebone carvings
Achilles's shield: described in Homer's *Iliad,* XVIII
Albrecht Dürer: Albrecht Dürer (1471-1528), German engraver and painter
Solomon islands . . . chronicled: discovered by Don Alvaro de Mendana in 1568 and chronicled by Cristóbal Suarez de Figueroa
Argo-Navis . . . Flying Fish: Navis, Cetus, and Hydrus are constellations in the Southern Hemisphere; *Flying Fish* is the ship in which Jason sought the Golden Fleece
fasces: bundle of rods, symbol of ancient Rome

Chapter LVIII. Brit

Brit is the minute yellow substance upon which the right whale feeds freely, out of danger from a sperm whale. Ishmael contemplates the stark contrasts of the ocean and the blissful life on land.

NOTES AND GLOSSARY:
brit: teeming spawn and young of fish, food for the right whale
terra incognita: *(Latin)* unknown land
Korah: one of those who rose up against Moses and Aaron and were swallowed by the earth, according to the Bible, Numbers 16:29-34

Chapter LIX. Squid

Daggoo sights a vast white mass, which upon examination proves to be the great live squid, whose sight few ships ever survive to report. This creature, said to be the largest animated thing in the ocean, has become the object of superstition and strange rumours.

NOTES AND GLOSSARY:

breaches: clears the water with its whole body

furlongs: each equalling 220 yards in length

Bishop Pontoppodan: Erik Pontoppidan (1698-1764), Danish Bishop of Bergen, in Norway, who wrote *Natural History of Norway* (1752-3)

cuttle fish: octopus

Anak: father of giants, according to the Bible, Numbers 13:33

Chapter LX. The Line

The whale-line is used to keep the hunting boat and the whale connected until the whale can be killed. This line feeds out through the boat at terrific speed after the harpoon, and care must be taken that when it flies out no one is killed or injured by kinks in it.

NOTES AND GLOSSARY:

Circassian: inhabitants of the east shore of the Black Sea. The people are proverbially beautiful

two hundred fathoms: twelve hundred feet

block: housing for pulley's sheaves

loggerhead: vertical post at the stern of a whaleboat

six burghers of Calais: King Edward III (1327-77) of England in 1347 promised to spare Calais if six persons of prominence offered themselves as sacrifices; six did offer themselves, but they were spared through the intercession of Queen Philippa

Mazeppa: hero of Byron's poem *Mazeppa,* who was bound to a wild horse

---

Chapter LXI. Stubb Kills a Whale

The next day after the sighting of the White Squid, Stubb kills a sperm whale.

NOTES AND GLOSSARY:

royal shrouds: ropes supporting sails fourth from the bottom on the mast

luff: sail nearer to the wind

spokes: of the wheel of the helm, but elsewhere the *Pequod* is said to have a tiller, not a wheel

Grenadier's steak: a steak from a human Grenadier, fit dish for a cannibal

spiracle: spout-hole

Chapter LXII. The Dart

Ishmael suggests that it would be more efficient to make the whaleboat's headman the harpooner too, so that his rest on the row out will provide him with the strength for a sure aim.

NOTES AND GLOSSARY:
disrated: demoted in rank

Chapter LXIII. The Crotch

The crotch does not hold the only harpoon aboard. A second iron, also attached to the whale line, is always ready and will follow the first out of the boat at great speed. The number of flying harpoons around a hunted whale is potentially great, and this is very hazardous.

Chapter LXIV. Stubb's Supper

Stubb's whale is secured with its tail towards the ship's prow. Around midnight Stubb eats a steak prepared by Fleece, the aged black cook. Meanwhile sharks tear viciously at the dead whale. Stubb berates Fleece for overcooking his delicacy and as a punishment makes him sermonise to the sharks.

NOTES AND GLOSSARY:
Hang-Ho: Hwang-ho
argosy: grand merchant vessel
capstan-head: windlass-bitts
knee-pans: knee caps
hatchings: hatches
they fetched Elijah: Elijah was carried to Heaven, according to the Bible, 2 Kings 2:11
lubber's hole: hole in the ship's top close to the mast for ease in ascent and descent
soused: pickled
Avast: stop

Chapter LXV. The Whale as a Dish

Ishmael recounts briefly the history of eating whales.

NOTES AND GLOSSARY:
Dunfermline: abbey near Edinburgh, in Scotland
oly-cooks: fried cakes
try watches: watches at trying time, when the blubber is boiled

Chapter XLVI. The Shark Massacre

Queequeg and another seaman strike long whaling-spades into the skulls of as many of the teeming sharks as possible to prevent damage to the whale's carcass.

NOTES AND GLOSSARY:
lash . . . a'lee: so that the ship heads into the wind
cutting stages: stages on which the men stood while cutting in

Chapter LXVII. Cutting In

Like an orange the whale is peeled, strip by strip. The strips are cut and lowered by machinery into the blubber-room area below decks.

NOTES AND GLOSSARY:
swayed: hoisted

Chapter LXVIII. The Blanket

The blubber of the whale is covered with a thin film. The blubber itself forms a kind of thick blanket that protects the fish in all climates from variations in temperature.

NOTES AND GLOSSARY:
Upper Mississippi: many earthworks in animal and bird shapes made by Indians are in this region
Agassiz: Louis Agassiz (1807-73), zoologist and geologist

Chapter LXIX. The Funeral

When the blubber has been stripped away, the peeled, headless body of the whale is dropped astern, with sharks and birds of prey swarming around.

NOTES AND GLOSSARY:
square roods: each equal to one-fourth of an acre

Chapter LXX. The Sphynx

Captain Ahab alone on deck speaks to the dead whale's head, as if it were a sphinx, containing the world's mysteries.

NOTES AND GLOSSARY:
Judith: the story of Judith slaying Holofernes is in the Book of Judith in the Apocrypha

bell: diving bell

Abraham: whose faith was proven by his willingness to sacrifice his son Isaac to God, according to the Bible, Genesis 22

Chapter LXXI. The *Jeroboam's* Story

The *Jeroboam* has been virtually taken over by a Shaker named Gabriel. Captain Mayhew tells Ahab about Moby Dick's killing of his chief mate, Macey. A letter addressed to Macey is returned to Ahab by Gabriel on the point of a pole.

NOTES AND GLOSSARY:

Jeroboam: besides the ship's name, the name of a wicked king, according to the Bible, 1 Kings 11-14

squaring her yards: putting her sails at right angles to the ship's heading

ranged abeam: came up at right angles to the ship's heading

main-topsail aback: the wind hitting it from the front

cabalistically cut: mysteriously cut

scaramouch: character in Italian *commedia dell'arte*, a coward and a braggart

Shakers: an offshoot sect of Quakers who believed in communal sharing of property and abstinence from sexual relations in preparation for the Millennium

seventh vial: the last destructive sign, in Revelation 16

Oceanica: collectively, the islands of the Pacific

main-royal mast-head: the lookout post there

pinny: perhaps 'tiny'

give way: begin to row

Chapter LXXII. The Monkey-Rope

A monkey-rope is a safety rope to protect a man who stands on the whale while the blubber is stripped away. Ishmael has one end of the rope round himself; the other is tied to Queequeg, who has the dangerous job of remaining on the turning whale in the bloody, shark-infested water.

NOTES AND GLOSSARY:

flensing: cutting-in

Highland costume: like a Scottish Highlander in his kilt

hard-scrabble: strenuous

lucifer matches: friction matches

calomel and jalop: both purgatives
tea-caddy: container for tea

Chapter LXXIII. Stubb and Flask Kill a Right Whale; and Then Have a Talk Over Him

---

Ahab orders the *Pequod* to take a right whale. Stubb and Flask kill one, and, as Fedallah recommended, the right whale's head is lifted on the opposite side to the sperm whale's.

NOTES AND GLOSSARY:
three rods: about fifty feet
smitten rock: smitten by Moses, in the Bible, Exodus 17
gamboge: yellow
oakum . . . boats: because the Devil was popularly believed to have hooves, not feet
the old flag-ship: heaven
soldadoes: soldiers
orlop: lowest deck level
double-darbies: iron shackles
Locke . . . Kant: John Locke (1632-1704), the English empirical philosopher, and Immanuel Kant (1724-1804), the German metaphysical philosopher
Parsee: Zoroastrian from Bombay; see 'Relevant ideas' in Part 1 of these notes
Laplandish: oriented to believe in superstitions

Chapter LXXIV. The Sperm Whale's Head—Contrasted View

The sperm whale's head is more symmetrical and has more character and dignity than the right whale's. The whale is blind directly in front and directly behind, and his brain must accommodate two separate worlds simultaneously. The jaw is lined with forty-two teeth.

NOTES AND GLOSSARY:
Euclid: Euclidian geometry
Herschel's great telescope: largest of its day, completed in 1789 by Sir William Herschel (1738-1822)
jib-boom: boom extending farthest forward on the ship

Chapter LXXV. The Right Whale's Head—Contrasted View

The right whale's head is slender, with a hare-lip and arched slats of bone instead of teeth. Ishmael contrasts the right and sperm whales' heads.

NOTES AND GLOSSARY:
galliot-toed: narrow, like this swift sailing-vessel
Mackinaw: Fort Mackinac on the Great Lakes
busks: stiffeners for corsets
great Haarlem organ: in Holland, a church organ with 5,000 pipes
Stoic: one with a stoic's resignation to fate and reliance on endurance and industry
Platonian: one with a lack of concern in worldly phenomena and a belief in ideal forms
Spinoza: a philosopher (1632-77) who devised a mathematical philosophy from first principles

Chapter LXXVI. The Battering-Ram

The sperm whale's brow rides high in the water when the whale is on the surface. The front of the whale is as invulnerable as a wall, so tough that the sharpest harpoon cannot pierce it.

NOTES AND GLOSSARY:
tow: hemp
Darien: Panama
salamander giants: able to endure the fires in the lofty regions of truth
youth . . . Sais: the youth is struck senseless and is forever melancholy thereafter—in a poem by the German Johann Christoph Friedrich von Schiller (1759-1805)

Chapter LXXVII. The Great Heidelburgh Tun

The most precious oil of the sperm whale comes from that massive part of the top of the whale's forehead called the 'case', or the great Heidelburgh Tun, which is full of spermaceti in its pure state.

NOTES AND GLOSSARY:
Heidelburgh Tun: wine cask holding about fifty thousand gallons
pelisse: fur or fur-lined coat

Chapter LXXVIII. Cistern and Buckets

After opening an area in the case, Tashtego begins emptying it, but the whole head breaks from its chains. Tashtego is only saved by the quick work of Queequeg, who pulls him free from the sinking mass.

NOTES AND GLOSSARY:
main-yard-arm: on the lowest yard on the mainmast

Niagara's Table-Rock: parts fell into the Niagara Falls in 1850
sanctum sanctorum: (Latin) holiest of holies

Chapter LXXIX. The Praire

Ishmael sets out to discover the character of the sperm whale by physiognomy and phrenology, but he declares that these sciences are like a 'passing fable', as are all other human sciences.

NOTES AND GLOSSARY:

Physiognomist:	student of human character as revealed by facial characteristics
Phrenologist:	student of personality traits as revealed in the shape of the skull
Pantheon:	a temple in Rome which has a hemispherical dome
Phidias's marble Jove:	by the Greek sculptor Phidias (fifth century BC), a statue long ago destroyed
jolly-boat:	little boat used as a hack-boat for small work
beadle:	parish constable
German emperors:	Holy Roman Emperors
Melancthon:	Philip Melancthon (1497-1560), a follower of Martin Luther
child-magian:	both child-like and wise, like a magus or wise man
Champollion:	Jean Francois Champollion (1790-1832), who deciphered Egyptian hieroglyphics by means of the Rosetta Stone
Sir William Jones:	Jones (1746-94) was an English philologist, orientologist, and jurist
Chaldee:	ancient Semitic language

Chapter LXXX. The Nut

Ishmael anatomises the interior of the sperm whale's head. Below the sperm, the junk, and the crater that supports them is a ten-inch-by-ten-inch cavity that holds the mere handful of the whale's brain.

NOTES AND GLOSSARY:

German conceit . . . skulls: Lorenz Oken (1779-1851) theorised that bones of the skull are analogous to vertebral columns

Chapter LXXXI. The *Pequod* Meets the *Virgin*

The *Jungfrau* (Virgin) has taken no whales, so Captain Derick De Deer boats over to borrow oil from the *Pequod*. When whales are

sighted De Deer forgets the charity given him by the *Pequod* and tries
to edge out the *Pequod*'s boats in the chase, to no avail. But the whale
taken by the *Pequod* proves too old and sinks.

NOTES AND GLOSSARY:

Jungfrau: *(German)* young woman, virgin
lamp-feeder: spouted vessel used to fill lamps with oil
pod: small group
Hindustan: Indian
Dog to it: stick to it, like a dog
Yarman: German
dogger: Dutch two-masted fishing vessel
white-ash breeze: breeze from the oars, made of white ash
German's quarter: forty-five degrees abaft the beam of the German's boat
butter-boxes: contemptuous for 'Dutchmen', since they love butter
tilbury: light, open, two-wheeled carriage
everlasting mail: men destined for death or Hell
weight of fifty atmospheres: fifty times sea-level pressure
'Canst thou . . . spear!': Ishmael's version of Job 41:7, 26-9, in the Bible
Xerxes' army: the powerful army headed by Xerxes that seized Athens in 480BC
crowding all sail: using every sail possible

Chapter LXXXII. The Honour and Glory of Whaling

Ishmael traces the ancient references to whales in mythology, the
Bible, and history to show the high esteem of whaling in the minds of
men.

NOTES AND GLOSSARY:

emblazoned: with a heraldic sign
Arkite: Canaanite tribe of what is now western Syria
Joppa . . . Jonah: see Chapter IX
St George . . . Dragon: always depicted as a land battle
'Thou art . . .sea': from the Bible, Ezekiel 32:2
griffin-like shape: half lion, half eagle
order of St George: Order of the Garter, (St George is its patron)
Hercules: in Greek mythology, he killed a sea monster while inside it
Crockett and Kit Carson: David Crockett (1786-1836) and Kit Carson (1809-68), American frontiersmen whose exploits were legendary

Shaster:	any one of the sacred writings of the Hindus
head off:	start

Chapter LXXXIII. Jonah Historically Regarded

Ishmael defends the factuality of the Jonah story against doubters, whom he rebukes for their foolish pride of reason.

NOTES AND GLOSSARY:

Arion:	seventh-century BC Greek poet, who was saved from drowning and carried to shore by a dolphin
Bishop Jebb:	John Jebb, Bishop of Limerick

French soldiers . . . Persian campaigners: Napoleon's soldiers
Bartholomew Diaz: rounded the Cape of Good Hope in 1486

Chapter LXXXIV. Pitchpoling

To kill a whale that keeps a swift horizontal flight, Stubb hurls a long spear attached to a rope into its life spot until it is dead.

NOTES AND GLOSSARY:
Cleopatra's barges . . . Actium: Cleopatra fled the battle of Actium in 31BC, leaving Anthony to fight the Romans

spigot:	stopper for a keg
Monongahela:	made on the Monongahela river in Pennsylvania

Chapter LXXXV. The Fountain

Ishmael contemplates whether the spoutings of whales be water or vapour, and he concludes that the spout is mist because the whale is profound and like the gods he always gives off semi-visible steam while thinking.

NOTES AND GLOSSARY:
sixteenth day of December, AD1851: the only indication of the date of composition in the work, given as 1850 in the English edition

rhyme:	rhythm
Pyrrho:	a sceptical Greek philosopher (fourth century BC)

Chapter LXXXVI. The Tail

Ishmael celebrates the powerful tail of the sperm whale.

NOTES AND GLOSSARY:

triune:	three-in-one

Titanism:	Titans were giants in Greek mythology
Eckerman . . . Goethe:	Johann Peter Eckermann's *Conversations with Gothe* (1836-48)
Angelo:	Michelangelo (1475-1564), Italian sculptor and painter, who painted the Sistine Chapel in Rome
zones:	waists
Dantean:	infernal, as in Dante's *Inferno*
Ptolemy . . . elephant:	reported in Plutarch's (*c*.AD46-*c*.120) *Morals*
King Juba:	North African of the first century BC
Free-Mason:	group with elaborate rituals and symbols, based on brotherhood and service.

Chapter LXXXVII. The Grand Armada

With pirates pursuing her and with whales ahead of her in flight, the *Pequod* passes through the Straits of Sunda. Free of pirates and in pursuit of the whales, Ishmael's boat comes to rest in the placid centre of the concentric circles of whales. There young are suckled and whales mate, but the scene is changed to a frenzied rush by the flailings of a wounded whale. The boat just escapes as all the whales charge the centre and dive.

NOTES AND GLOSSARY:

Bally:	Bali
Propontis:	Sea of Marmara
proas:	outrigger canoes with sails
kentledge:	ballast
rowels:	spurs
King Porus' elephants:	Porus was defeated by Alexander the Great in 327BC
Gulf-weed:	kind of seaweed
Arnold . . . Saratoga:	Arnold was conspicuous for bravery at the battle of Saratoga, 7 October 1777
Dardanelles:	strait connecting the Mediterranean to the Sea of Marmara

Chapter LXXXVIII. Schools and Schoolmasters

Ishmael tells about the two kinds of schools in which sperm whales swim: the school of females and the school of males.

NOTES AND GLOSSARY:

Ottoman:	Turk
en bon point:	*enbonpoint (French),* plumpness
Bashaw:	Pasha, Turkish title of honour

Solomon . . . concubines: according to the Bible, 1 Kings 11, three
hundred concubines and seven hundred wives

memoirs of Vidocq: supposedly by Eugène Francois Vidocq
(1775-1857), a Parisian detective

Daniel Boone: an American frontiersman (1734-1820) of
legendary exploits

Chapter LXXXIX. Fast-Fish and Loose-Fish

A 'fast-fish' is defined as any fish attached by any means to a boat or
ship or to a waif or any other symbol or possession of a particular
ship. A 'loose-fish' is game for anyone who can catch it.

NOTES AND GLOSSARY:

Justinian's Pandects: the sixth-century codification of the Roman law
by the Emperor Justinian

Coke-upon-Littleton: a commentary by Sir Edward Coke (1552-1634)
on a work on property law by Sir Thomas
Littleton (1422-81)

doxology: hymn of praise to the Christian Trinity

crim. con. case: criminal conversation case, that is, adultery

Temple of Philistines: according to the Bible, Judges 16:29, this was
supported by two pillars

Chapter XC. Heads or Tails

An old English law states that the King should have the head and the
Queen the tail of each whale.

NOTES AND GLOSSARY:

'De balena . . . caudam': *(Latin)* 'It indeed suffices , concerning the
whale, if the king should have the head, and the
queen the tail'

Cinque Ports: five ports on the coast of the English Channel with
an agreement for mutual privileges and protection

fobbing: pocketing

Blackstone: *Commentaries on the Laws of England (1765-9)*
by Sir William Blackstone (1723-80)

Duke of Wellington: Arthur Wellesley, first Duke of Wellington
(1769-1852), victor of the battle of Waterloo

three kingdoms: comprising Great Britain

Plowdon: Edmund Plowden, the sixteenth-century English
jurist

William Prynne: Prynne (1600-69) was author of *Aurum Reginae,
or Concerning Queen Gold (1668)*

Chapter XCI. The *Pequod* Meets the *Rose-Bud*

Stubb ingeniously cheats the French whaler *Rose-Bud* out of a stinking, dead whale full of valuable ambergris.

NOTES AND GLOSSARY:

fetor:	stench
Sir T. Browne:	Sir Thomas Browne (1605-82), English physician and author of *Religio Medici* (1643) and *Pseudodoxia Epidemica* (1646)
Crappoes:	from French *crapauds*: toads
stem-piece:	between the knight-heads, strengthens that part of the ship through which the bowsprit passes
head-boards:	bows
Guernsey-man:	from Guernsey, a French-speaking Channel Island
round-house:	separate housing built over the deck as a cabin
watch-seals:	watch fobs
St Jago:	a Cape Verde island

Chapter XCII. Ambergris

Ambergris, used in making perfume, is found in the bowels of sick whales.

NOTES AND GLOSSARY:

pastiles:	pastilles, tablets for deodorising
Brandreth's pills:	used to alleviate constipation
St Paul . . . incorruption:	in the Bible, I Corinthians 15:42-3
Paracelsus:	Philippus Aureolus Paracelsus (1493?-1541), Swiss physician and alchemist

Chapter XCIII. The Castaway

The small cabin-boy Pip replaces an oarsman in Stubb's boat, but he is unsuited to the work. After two unfortunate outings, Pip jumps out of the boat in fright and is left on the open ocean, where his isolation and fear drive him mad. He is later picked up by the ship.

NOTES AND GLOSSARY:

gold-beater's skin:	thin sheets of beaten gold
spoke:	called out to

Chapter XCIV. A Squeeze of the Hand

Ishmael squeezes by hand the congealing spermaceti from the Heidelburgh Tun, and he contemplates its effect of allaying ill will.

NOTES AND GLOSSARY:
Constantine's bath: in the Baptistery of San Giovanni in Laterano in Rome.
Paracelsan: Paracelsus, the sixteenth-century Swiss alchemist
Berkshire marble: quarried in Berkshire, Massachusetts
Louis le Gros: Louis the Fat, Louis VI (1108-37) of France
horse-pieces: portable, rectangular chunks of blubber

Chapter XCV. The Cassock

The 'grandissimus' is peeled, then dried, and used as clothing by the mincer, who thinly cuts the blubber into the boiling pot.

NOTES AND GLOSSARY:
Queen Maachah . . . Kings: reported in the Bible, 1 Kings 15:11/13
grandissimus: besides the whale part, Latin: the grandest fellow
canonicals: priest's vestments

Chapter XCVI. The Try-Works

As the sailors sit around the ghostly light of the trying fire, Ishmael stands at the helm. His head fills with visions and he comes to his senses only just in time to prevent the vessel from flying into the wind.

NOTES AND GLOSSARY:
battened: fastened closed
cycloid: curved line traced by a point on a circle rolling along a straight line
plethoric: huge
left wing . . . judgement: at Judgement Day those damned to hell stand on the left hand of God, according to the Bible, Matthew 25
Canaris: Constantine Canaris from Hydra used this tactic in 1822
Tartarean shapes: as if from Tartarus, the hell of Greek mythology
brought by the lee: turned toward the lee side of the ship
Man of Sorrows: Christ
truest of all books: Ecclesiastes, in the Bible
Cowper . . . Rousseau: William Cowper (1731-1800) and Edward Young (1683-1765), English poets; Blaise Pascal (1623-62), French mathematician, philosopher and theologian; Jean Jacques Rousseau (1712-78), French writer and political philosopher: all were 'Romantics' who brooded on the deep and subtle spiritual truths of natural existence

Rabelais:	Francois Rabelais (1494-1553), French physician, philosopher, and author of *Gargantua and Pantagruel*

Chapter XCVII. The Lamp

The off-duty watch sleep with lamps burning. Other sailors must move in darkness; the whalemen move always in light.

NOTES AND GLOSSARY:

early grass butter: butter made from the milk of cows who feed on spring grass

---

Chapter XCVIII. Stowing Down and Clearing Up

Newly-made oil is poured, still hot, into six-barrel casks. When cooled, the casks are lowered into the bowels of the ship.

NOTES AND GLOSSARY:

Shadrach, Meshach, and Abednego:	condemned to death in a fiery furnace, but remained unharmed according to the Bible, Daniel 3
ex officio:	*(Latin)* as part of the duties of his office
ley:	lye, a strong alkaline solution
Holland:	linen
metempsychosis:	transmigration of the soul out of the body, originally an Egyptian idea

---

Chapter XCIX. The Doubloon

Ahab scrutinises the doubloon on the mainmast, seeing himself in each image and the coin as the globe. Then Starbuck, Stubb, Flask, the Old Manxman, Queequeg and Fedallah each react to the coin. While the others have interpreted the coin, Pip has looked on, and now interprets what he has seen in his own way. Clearly each person sees in the coin something that defines himself.

NOTES AND GLOSSARY:

Pactolus:	river in Turkey
Belshazzar's awful writing:	the ominous handwriting on the wall, according to the Bible, Daniel 5
nine fathoms:	fifty-four feet: an exaggeration
Corlear's Hook:	on Manhattan Island
Popayan:	city in Colombia
moidores . . . joes:	Spanish and Portuguese coins

Golconda:	city in India, famous for its diamond mines
Bowditch:	Nathaniel Bowditch (1773-1838), compiler of *New American Practical Navigator* (1802), a standard nautical handbook
Daboll's arithmetic:	Nathan Daboll, *Complete Schoolmaster's Assistant* (1779)
Massachusetts calendar:	Massachusetts almanac
Jimimi:	Gemini
oakum . . . pumps:	in popular superstition the Devil had hooves, not feet, so to wear human shoes he had to stuff the toes
Murray's Grammar:	Lindley Murray, *The English Grammar* (1795)
resurrection:	raising of the dead at the Last Judgement
God . . . blackberrying:	God observes man going astray (that is, man 'going blackberrying')

Chapter C. Leg and Arm: the *Pequod,* of Nantucket, Meets the *Samuel Enderby,* of London.

Captain Boomer of the *Samuel Enderby* describes how he lost his arm on account of a confrontation with Moby Dick. When Boomer says he will not chase that whale again, Ahab excitedly resumes his quest.

NOTES AND GLOSSARY:

quarter-boat:	boat suspended from the quarter-deck
runabout:	sailor's jacket
huzzar's:	hussar's; a hussar was a member of a light cavalry regiment
cleets:	cleats
trim dish:	maintain even keel
down . . . Lima's tower:	like a tower in earthquake-prone Lima
sucking fish:	one with a suction cup on its head for clinging to other fish

---

Chapter CI. The Decanter

Ishmael celebrates the presence of Nantucketers in the whaling trade, and he describes the good cheer he received when visiting the *Samuel Enderby* long after Ahab's visit.

NOTES AND GLOSSARY:

Post-Captain:	full-grade captain
flip:	spiced liquor

Chapter CII. A Bower in the Arsacides

Ishmael describes what little he learned from examining and measuring a skeleton of a great sperm whale revered in a temple in the Arsacidean Islands.

NOTES AND GLOSSARY:

untagging . . . hose: loosening the laces that bind the hose to the jacket

poke or bag: stomach skin

Tranque . . . Arsacides: the Arsacides are a group of islands in the Solomons; Tranque is near southern Chile; Tranquo is fictitious

vertù: *virtù (Italian)* curios

Damocles: a man of Syracuse who was forced to eat at a banquet with a sword hung by a hair over his head, symbolic of the precarious life of a king

Icy Glen: in western Massachusetts

Chapter CIII. Measurement of the Whale's Skeleton

A sperm whale of the largest magnitude will weigh at least ninety tons, but Ishmael's measurements of the whale's skeleton in the Arsacides give very little idea of the whale itself.

NOTES AND GLOSSARY:

Pompey's Pillar: a column near Alexandria

Chapter CIV. The Fossil Whale

Surveying the fossil remains of ancient whales, Ishmael concludes that whales predate and will probably postdate man on earth.

NOTES AND GLOSSARY:

Johnson: Samuel Johnson's *Dictionary of the English Language* (1755)

pre-adamite: before the biblical Adam

Saturn's grey chaos: Saturn's reign in Greek mythology

Methuselah: lived 969 years, according to the Bible, Genesis 5:27

Shem: oldest of Noah's three sons, according to the Bible, Genesis 5:32

antemosaic: predating Moses

John Leo: Johannes Leo (*c.* 1494-1552), a Moorish explorer from Spain who wrote *Description of Africa* (1526)

Chapter CV. Does the Whale's Magnitude Diminish?—Will He Perish?

Ishmael maintains that the whale is 'immortal in his species, however perishable in his individuality'.

NOTES AND GLOSSARY:

Pliny:	Pliny the elder, the first-century Roman
Aldrovandus:	Ulisse Aldrovandi (1522-1605), Italian naturalist
Thames Tunnel:	tunnel under the Thames, from Wapping to Rotherhithe in east London, opened in 1843
Banks . . . naturalists:	Sir Joseph Banks (1743-1820) and Daniel Charles Solander (1736-82), naturalists who accompanied Captain James Cook on his voyage around the world (1768-71)
Smithfield:	London's cattle market
yokes:	pairs
cachelot:	*(French)* sperm whale
Harto:	Garcias ab Horto, physician to the Portuguese viceroy at Goa, India, as cited in Browne's *Pseudodoxia Epidemica,* Book VI, Chapter 6
Semiramis:	legendary Assyrian queen, builder of Babylon
Porus:	defeated by Alexander the Great in 327BC
Hannibal:	Carthaginian general who crossed the Alps with elephants
New Holland:	Australia

Chapter CVI. Ahab's Leg

Ahab orders the carpenter to repair his untrustworthy ivory leg, shattered during his return from the *Samuel Enderby*.

NOTES AND GLOSSARY:

thwart:	seat
Grand-Lama-like:	like the Dalai Lama, head of Buddhism in Tibet
transpire:	be spoken of

Chapter CVII. The Carpenter

The carpenter will repair anything aboard the whaler. He works instinctively, always talking to himself.

NOTES AND GLOSSARY:

Saturn:	traditionally associated with melancholy and genius

tree-nails:	long, wooden pins
athwartships:	at right angles to the fore-and-aft line
belaying pin:	peg set in the rail for fastening ropes
top-blocks:	pulleys used to manoeuvre the top-mast
multum in parvo:	*(Latin)* much in little
quicksilver:	mercury
hartshorn:	ammonia

Chapter CVIII. Ahab and the Carpenter: The Deck—First Night Watch

Ahab speaks with the carpenter as he is fitted for his new ivory leg. His talk about making a giant and about the sensation of a leg where there is none confuses the carpenter, who compares Ahab to a heron that one should not follow into deep water.

NOTES AND GLOSSARY:

ferule and buckle-screw: metal tip and screw for the buckle

Prometheus:	Greek mythological figure who was so excellent a craftsman that he made men from clay
old Adam:	sinfulness
Praetorians:	the elite (becoming very rich, powerful, and corrupt) guard of the Roman Emperor

resurrection fellow: angel who blows the trumpet for the Last Judgement

taking altitudes:	as if with a quadrant

Chapter CIX. Ahab and Starbuck in the Cabin

Starbuck is berated for suggesting to Ahab that the holds should be emptied to fix a leak. Ahab even threatens Starbuck with a musket, but finally Ahab relents and orders the holds emptied to repair the leak.

NOTES AND GLOSSARY:

Bashee Isles:	Batan Islands

Up Burtons and break out: set up the tackle and take out the casks from the hold

Chapter CX. Queequeg and His Coffin

Queequeg's illness, contracted while he was taking casks out of the hold, brings him so near death that he orders a coffin to be made and fits it out for his burial. When he recovers, he makes the coffin his sea-chest and carves on it the signs tattooed on his body.

NOTES AND GLOSSARY:
puncheons:	casks
tierce:	forty-two-gallon barrel
shooks of staves:	sets of staves, prepared pieces of wood for making barrels
demijohn:	large bottle
endless end:	death
Zoroaster:	see 'Relevant ideas' in Part 1 of these notes
leeway:	distance the ship is pushed to leeward by the wind
Lackaday islands:	Laccadive Islands in the Arabian Sea
Antilles:	West Indies, common term for Paradise
Rig-a-dig:	imitative of the sound of a tambourine

Chapter CXI. The Pacific

Contrasted are Ishmael's wonder at the first sight of the Pacific Ocean and Ahab's steely concentration on the Japanese Cruising Ground, where he is to meet the White Whale.

NOTES AND GLOSSARY:
undulations . . . St John:	Ephesian legend told by St Augustine
Potter's Fields:	probably those bought with the thirty pieces of silver that Judas Iscariot earned by betraying Jesus, according to the Bible, Matthew 27:6-10
Magian:	like a magus, or wise man
Abraham:	patriarch of the Jews
Pan:	pastoral god, whose name, Greek for 'all', implies his universal presence

Chapter CXII. The Blacksmith

The blacksmith Perth had a disastrous life ashore and now makes his work his life and the ship his tomb.

NOTES AND GLOSSARY:
ring bolts:	bolts driven into the deck with rings attached
pike-heads:	prongs of the blubber-pike used to move blubber about the deck
Bottle Conjurer:	the djinn of the bottle, from the *Arabian Nights*

Chapter CXIII. The Forge

Ahab helps Perth the blacksmith to forge a harpoon's head from the strongest metals. Tashtego, Daggoo, and Queequeg give their blood to temper the blade. Ahab fits the head on to a hickory pole.

NOTES AND GLOSSARY:

iron-wood:	kind of hardwood
Mother Carey's chickens:	petrels
gaffs:	hooks
fusee:	fuse
Icy Sea:	polar sea
tow-line:	whale line
Three Fates:	Clotho, Lachesis, and Atropos, three sisters in Greek mythology, all involved in the work and destruction of weaving

Chapter CXIV. The Gilder

The first glimpse of the Japanese Cruising Ground is calm and puts everyone in a meditative mood.

Chapter CXV. The *Pequod* Meets the *Bachelor*

The *Bachelor* is full of oil and returning to Nantucket, with her crew dancing on deck with native women.

NOTES AND GLOSSARY:

signals, ensigns, and jacks: all available flags
top-mast cross-trees: at the head of each top-mast
black fish: among the whales classified in Chapter XXXII
pulling down . . . Bastille: revolutionaries pulling down this prison in Paris after the beginning of the French Revolution in 1789

Chapter CXVI. The Dying Whale

Ahab marvels that the whale he kills turns his head towards the sun while dying, but turns away from it after the moment of death.

NOTES AND GLOSSARY:

Manilla isles: the Philippines
Niger's unknown source: unknown until the early nineteenth century
all-quickening: life-giving
imminglings: mixings

Chapter CXVII. The Whale Watch

While waiting through the night in the whaleboat with the dead whale, Ahab has a dream; Fedallah says that before Ahab can die he must see two hearses on the sea, the first not made by mortal hands, the wood of the other grown in America. Further, before Ahab can die, Fedallah himself must die, and only hemp can kill Ahab.

NOTES AND GLOSSARY:
Asphallites: the Dead Sea

Chapter CXVIII. The Quadrant

Ahab casts the quadrant to the deck and tramples it. He resolves to navigate by other means than by the sun.

NOTES AND GLOSSARY:

effulgences:	outpouring streams of light
dead reckoning:	from a previous reliable fixed point the position is determined by courses taken and previous speed accomplished
square in:	pull sails perpendicular to the heading
three Horatii:	three legendary brothers (triplets) chosen to fight three brothers from the opposing side in strife between Rome and Alba
knight-heads:	uprights in the bow
sea-coal:	coal

Chapter CXIX. The Candles

A wave staves in Ahab's whaleboat. In the storm electricity makes the masts seem like flames. Ahab worships the lightening and terrifies the crew by his ability to command the flames.

NOTES AND GLOSSARY:

perilous fluid:	electricity
Mene . . . Upharsin:	prophetic handwriting on the wall of the King of Babylon, according to the Bible, Daniel 5
Herculaneum:	near Pompeii, where bodies caught during the eruption of the volcano in AD79 have been preserved
as Persian:	like a Parsee

Chapter CXX. The Deck Towards the End of the First Night Watch

Ahab tells Starbuck to lash only what is necessary but not to strike anything in the storm.

NOTES AND GLOSSARY:

band:	canvas strip sewn to the top third of a sail with attached ropes for reefing
half-stranded:	half unravelled

strike:	lower
sky-sail-poles:	extensions of the masts
working:	moving
table-lands:	plateaux
smack:	small fishing vessel

Chapter CXXI. Midnight—the Forecastle Bulwarks

As Stubb and Flask lash the anchors, Flask reminds Stubb that once he said that Ahab's ships should be insured for an extra fee.

NOTES AND GLOSSARY:

crown of the anchor:	where the arms meet the shank
swallow-tail:	coat
beaver:	beaver hat

Chapter CXXII. Midnight Aloft—Thunder and Lightening

Tashtego, lashing the main-top-sail yard, orders the thunder to stop; he says the crew would rather have rum than thunder.

Chapter CXXIII. The Musket

The storm turns the compass of the ship around, so that it heads back into clear weather. Starbuck, going to tell Ahab about the good weather, contemplates killing Ahab with a musket in order to stop the destructive quest; but he does not do so.

NOTES AND GLOSSARY:

preventer tackles:	used to relieve pressure
bent:	attached
storm-trysail:	triangular sail spread fore-and-aft in storms

Chapter CXXIV. The Needle

Ahab realises that the calm-weather course is a result of the turned compass. He fixes the compass and continues his former course after Moby Dick.

NOTES AND GLOSSARY:

produced:	streamed forth
loadstone:	magnetic stone
sharp:	edge
juggling:	deceiving
level loadstone:	compass

Chapter CXXV. The Log and Line

Ahab orders the long-neglected log and line to be used to compute the ship's position. Mad Pip is given refuge by Ahab, and the Manxman proclaims both to be mad.

NOTES AND GLOSSARY:
hit the world: described the world precisely

Chapter CXXVI. The Life-Buoy

In the dark wild cries are heard. Later rising to his watch, a sailor falls overboard. The lifebuoy is cast after him, but he is not found. How is the lifebuoy to be replaced?

NOTES AND GLOSSARY:

pay over:	cover with pitch
bandbox:	light box for hats
job-shop:	shop where miscellaneous work is performed
Aroostook:	from Aroostook County in Maine
Cruppered:	fitted-out behind, as with a horse's trappings
Turk's head:	braided or knotted

Chapter CXXVII. The Deck

The carpenter turns Queequeg's coffin into a lifebuoy, and Ahab is struck by the symbol of life transformed from that of death.

NOTES AND GLOSSARY:

Titans:	giants of Greek mythology
grave-digger . . . play:	Shakespeare's *Hamlet,* V.1
musical glasses:	an instrument comprising different lengths of glass that make music when struck

Chapter CXXVIII. The *Pequod* Meets the *Rachel*

Captain Gardiner of the *Rachel* tries to enlist Ahab's help in searching for a whaleboat crew last seen pursuing Moby Dick. Even though the crew contains Gardiner's own son, Ahab is obdurate and, warning Gardiner off his ship, he continues his quest.

NOTES AND GLOSSARY:

binnacle watch:	chronometer
Rachel . . . children:	from the Bible, Jeremiah 31:15, quoted in Matthew 2:18

Chapter CXXIX. The Cabin

Ahab bids farewell to Pip and orders him to stay in the cabin.

NOTES AND GLOSSARY:
seventy-fours: great warships with seventy-four guns

Chapter CXXX. The Hat

Ahab, impatient to see Moby Dick himself, makes a basket by which he is raised beside the royal mast to look out. A black sea-hawk whirls screaming about his head, picks up his hat, takes it far out to sea and drops it.

NOTES AND GLOSSARY:
cabin-scuttle: stair to the cabin
pin: belaying pin, placed on rail for fastening ropes
Tarquin: Lucius Tarquinius Priscus, made a king in 616BC

Chapter CXXXI. The *Pequod* Meets the *Delight*

The *Delight's* whaleboat has been stove by Moby Dick. To the captain of the *Delight,* Ahab shows his harpoon and swears to plant it in Moby Dick.

NOTES AND GLOSSARY:
taffrail: rail at the stern

Chapter CXXXII. The Symphony

Ahab, leaning over the calm sea, sheds a tear, which Starbuck takes as a sign of humanity. The two talk, and Starbuck tries to dissuade Ahab from his plan. Ahab feels that some great power is driving him onwards and he cannot stop.

NOTES AND GLOSSARY:
Samson's chest . . . sleep: Samson was sleeping when Delilah betrayed him, according to the Bible, Judges 16:4-20
Guinea Coast: west coast of central Africa
cindered apple: like the legendary apples of Sodom, described by Flavius Josephus (AD37-*c*.100), the Jewish historian and soldier, in *The History of the Jewish War*, IV, VIII, 4, 484
cozzening: cozening, cheating
Albicore: tunny fish

Chapter CXXXIII. The Chase—First Day

Ahab is first to sight the White Whale. The wily whale breaks up Ahab's boat, and Ahab is saved from the whale only by Starbuck's manoeuvring of the *Pequod*. Ahab does not claim the doubloon, but he leaves it on the mast for the next day's hunt.

NOTES AND GLOSSARY:

dog-vane:	swinging cloth in the shape of a truncated cone which catches the wind and thus shows its direction
sail . . . shortened:	reefed
judgment claps:	as on Judgement Day
alow and aloft:	set all sails
luff:	turn towards the wind
shiver her:	bring her into the wind so that the sails shiver
argosy:	grand merchant vessel
Jupiter . . . Europa:	in Greek mythology Europa was carried to Crete by a snow-white bull, which was Jupiter in disguise
Virginia's Natural Bridge:	the limestone wonder in western Virginia
to stern:	to back up
Antiochus's elephants:	in the Apocrypha; see 7 Maccabees 6

Chapter CXXXIV. The Chase—Second Day

Moby Dick breaches, and boats are launched. Three harpoons are fixed in the whale, but the whale crosses the lines and breaks up two boats, then dashes itself against Ahab's. Fedallah is killed, and Ahab recognises that one term of the prophecy has been fulfilled.

NOTES AND GLOSSARY:

breaches:	clears water with its whole body

Chapter CXXXV. The Chase—Third Day

Ahab takes one last look at the broad ocean. Two boats are quickly destroyed by the whale, and Ahab's harpoon thrust is arrested when he sees the torn body of Fedallah on Moby Dick's side. Still pursuing the whale, Ahab is aghast when Moby Dick turns to charge the *Pequod*. Unable to help, Ahab watches the whale break through his ship's side. In despair Ahab hurls his harpoon, but he is caught in a flying turn of his own hempen rope and dragged to his death. The *Pequod* sinks as Tashtego calmly nails a red flag to the mast.

NOTES AND GLOSSARY:

quarter:	forty-five degrees abaft the beam
gold-beaten out:	beaten out like very thin sheets of gold
three points:	about thirty-three degrees
into the wind's eye:	directly into the wind
shallop's stem:	stem of a small light open boat
knotted hamper:	tangled harpoon lines
Monadnock:	mountain in southern New Hampshire
bowstring:	strangle
Fata Morgana:	mirage

Epilogue

Only Ishmael escapes from the destruction of the *Pequod;* all other hands are lost. Queequeg's coffin, now a lifebuoy, saves him, and he is picked up by the *Rachel,* still searching for its lost whaleboat crew.

NOTES AND GLOSSARY:

Ixion:	in Greek mythology, punished by being bound to a fiery wheel in Hades
Rachel . . . orphan:	the biblical story is in Jeremiah 31

Part 3

Commentary

Nature, purpose and achievement

Moby Dick is the first American fictional work that may, without qualification, be called a work of the first rank in world literature. Although it is about whaling, it is not just a sea story. It is a long, fictional work in prose, but it is not a traditional novel. While it borrows from their conventions, it is not properly an epic or a tragedy. It is close to being an encyclopedia of a special kind, called an 'anatomy', or minute dissection of a whole area of human life—whale hunting. But *Moby Dick* does not really belong to any single genre of literature, though it borrows from many. Like any work of genius it abides by its own rules, examining the profundities of life.

Moby Dick is also Melville's first great work of fiction, and it is his best. Like his other works, it draws not only on his own experience but also on his vast reading. It was written at that particularly fruitful time when Melville lived near to and often conversed with Nathaniel Hawthorne, whose melancholy contemplation of human evil doubtless contributed to certain themes in *Moby Dick*. Like Hawthorne's novels and stories, *Moby Dick* is fraught with symbolism: its colours, objects, characters and actions all convey significant meanings. Like Hawthorne, Melville emphasises the moral significance of human actions, the isolation of crazed intellect, and the sinister forces that operate in the world and in man. But unlike Hawthorne, Melville provides a narrator in Ishmael who both playfully explores the most far-fetched meanings for the smallest details, and detachedly laughs at himself for doing so. Ishmael's strangely comical attitude is mixed with a delight in antiquarian details for their own sakes. Through him, Melville can provide detachment both from the tragical story of Ahab and from profound significance that no man can fully comprehend.

Relation of background

Ahab is a hero of the type Carlyle discussed in his essay *On Heroes and Hero-Worship*. He is a titanic figure, whose intellect and will-power make him a natural leader. But his obsession about killing

Moby Dick is clearly an encroaching madness. As Ahab gets closer and closer to the prey, his madness increases. Finally he cannot be reclaimed by any appeal, and his last despairing thrust of the harpoon is both useless and suicidal. Ahab tries to kill a brute in revenge for the loss of his leg, but the White Whale's malevolent intelligence and destructiveness clearly show him to be a conscious force. Ahab's intuition that Moby Dick is almost a universal principle rather than a mere mortal fish is in the end shared by the reader.

Ahab associates himself with demonic powers, the Devil, and darkness, and he actually challenges the powers of reason, humanity, and the light of the sun and fire. Although a Quaker by background, Ahab is a warrior of evil through his association with the White Whale. He destroys his crew and himself and leaves his family alone.

In contrast to Ahab's wilful pursuit of Moby Dick is the harpooners' seeming unconcern for the course of events. Pagan, they are all fatalists and almost cheerfully follow wherever Ahab leads. They represent the various kinds of noble savage represented in literature and art. They provide a stark contrast to the Christian crew; they are supermen, in tune with the elements and with their trade. But they are largely unconscious. Their heroism is of a primeval sort. They live and die with a kind of simple dignity.

The one harpooner who is not a traditional type of noble savage is Fedallah, the Parsee. His religion separates him from the rest of the crew. He believes in the power of good over evil. He scorns Ahab when Ahab spurns the sun and fire which he holds sacred. He believes in prophecy, and his prophecies all come true. Through this reclusive, almost diabolical harpooner, the whole framework of Zoroastrianism can operate in the novel. No search for an ordinary whale, the quest for Moby Dick is about man's search for ultimate meaning in conflict with the powers that govern the universe.

Ishmael provides an Emersonian viewpoint through which the story of Ahab can be interpreted. Always seeking for transcendental meanings behind everything, Ishmael usually concludes reveries with his admission of his own intellectual inadequacies or with a comparison so outlandish as to make the reader smile. Ishmael's sane judgement about the insufficiency of man's intellect spares him from the pride of Ahab. Yet Ishmael is not sceptical about true values. He has been raised as a Presbyterian. He believes in Providence, or God's Plan, behind all events. Detached, he faces the mysteries with an open, analogy-forming mind and with wit and humour. Ironically he is in the right place at the right time both to be cast out of Ahab's doomed whaleboat and to avail himself of Queequeg's coffin-turned-lifebuoy. His own survival is a sign of the 'Providential' structure of the book.

Emersonian idealism is opposed throughout the book by the sinister dangers that confront dreamers in the active life. Meditation can mean dishonour or death, if improperly governed. Whenever peace and value seem to be ascendant in the work, some atrocity breaks the spell—for example, the whale with the cutting spade scattering destruction among the gentle whales in 'The Grand Armada'. This is not to say that moments of peace are not valued. They are. But they do not last. Further, truths discovered one day must be modified the next. Yet even in the face of this apparent relativism, Ishmael's faith in the ultimate triumph of goodness in the world comes to bear fruit.

Structure

Ishmael's own account is the envelope for all that takes place. He opens the book with 'Call me Ishmael' and closes it with the account of his rescue. Within this envelope is the story of Ahab's pursuit of the whale. But this story does not proceed without interruptions and digressions. Most of the central chapters deal with information and background about whaling. These chapters are generally necessary for understanding the situations to come, though some are clearly amplifications of major themes or playful interludes. The book oscillates between chapters of information and chapters about Ahab's quest, and the final chapters are wholly devoted to the struggle between Ahab and Moby Dick.

Ishmael's voice is not always dominant. Many chapters are in dramatic form; some do not have Ishmael as the narrator. At times Ishmael seems to be Melville himself. Yet the tone of presentation is consistent throughout. With broad variation between high tragedy and low comedy, between satire and praise of democracy, between profound meditation and simple description, *Moby Dick,* nevertheless, is governed by the simple mentality of Ishmael. He has been called the true hero of the novel

Style

Plot

Since Ishmael does not develop as a character in *Moby Dick,* his story is relatively simple to tell. He ships aboard the *Pequod,* a whaler, observes at first hand the action aboard, and in the final bout with the whale is miraculously saved from death. Ahab's story is somewhat more difficult to relate than Ishmael's because it involves the past. Ahab's leg was taken off by Moby Dick, and, in the resulting anguish,

Ahab determined to take revenge on the whale. Concealing his motive from the crew until the *Pequod* is at sea, Ahab finally reveals his quest and gains the approbation of all the crew except Starbuck. Nevertheless, Ahab becomes increasingly melancholic as he nears the whale's ground. He admits madness, and his actions show him to be mad. He pursues the whale in spite of all natural and supernatural signs of warning. Even after the loss of the *Pequod,* Ahab pursues the whale and is killed. The effects of this simple, tragical plot are heightened by the emphasis Ishmael places on the deep meanings of all events and portents. Repetition and amplification for over a hundred chapters cause the reader to consider Moby Dick not just as a whale but as a gigantic symbol.

Narration

Ishmael's first-person narration provides the means by which a relatively simple story becomes a significant masterpiece. Learned, observant and meditative, Ishmael reports all that is necessary for absolute clarity of understanding of events. He introduces the reader to the complex world of whaling gradually. His contemplation of, say, the whiteness of the whale, is full of curious lore from historical records and from legends from the trade of whaling. Unlike Father Mapple's sermon on Jonah, Ishmael's account is not overtly didactic or sermonic. Moral meaning is to be found in *Moby Dick* through struggling with the actions and ideas presented, not through accepting certain statements of truth scattered through the book. Ishmael reports the reactions of others to events, and so gains additional points of view, as when Pip or Fedallah are seen to react verbally or with a facial expression to Ahab's actions.

Characterisation

For the most part, characterisation in *Moby Dick* is purposely flat. The only rounded characters are Ahab, Ishmael, and Starbuck. Only Ahab and Starbuck actually develop. The effect of this shaping of character is that Ahab's quest and personality are heightened or accentuated. Stubb, Flask, Tashtego, Daggoo, and (with certain qualifications) Queequeg are known from their first introductions. Some characters, such as Bulkington, are known only as symbols. Others, such as Mrs Hosea Hussey, are satirical portraits. Most have efficient roles to perform; examples are Archy, the carpenter, and the Old Manx Sailor, though the last two here are respectively symbolical and superstitious too. Characters in the prolonged anecdotes of the *Town-Ho* and the *Jeroboam* are interesting, even enigmatical, but not fully developed. The flat characters, that is, characters who do not develop and thus have minor roles to play, are usually character types. For example, Daggoo is a noble savage and Aunt Charity is a do-gooder with no apprehension of the lives she is trying to better. To label *Moby Dick* as an allegory on account of its flat characterisation would be a grave mistake, because Melville, through Ishmael, provides different characters for different purposes; relatively few characters have the representational qualities of characters in an allegory, a literary form in which all characters are personified abstractions.

Irony

Moby Dick is full of irony. It is ironical that the *Pequod* is so decorated with whalebone that it is almost like the whales that it must hunt. It is ironical that a lifebuoy, a sign of life, should have been made from a coffin, a sign of death. It is ironical that the colour white should be associated with evil, when for centuries it has been associated with good. Examples of verbal, situational and symbolical irony abound. Sometimes the irony is used for satire, as when Aunt Charity's tea-caddy is sent aboard for cannibals. Sometimes it is tragic, as in Ahab's name, which signifies a wicked life and evil end. The irony and symbolism work hand in hand, since Ishmael's humanity triumphs over his missionary zeal in dealing with Queequeg and since the brotherhood of Queequeg and Ishmael bears fruit after Queequeg is dead.

Symbolism

Although not an allegory, *Moby Dick* is full of symbols, objects, persons, and actions that are powerfully charged with meanings. The White Whale is perhaps the most enigmatical symbol in the work. To limit its meaning to life, or truth, or evil, or mindless nature, or a projection of the male principle, or raw intelligence, would be unfair. The whale is all these things and more; most of all the White Whale is itself. In 'The Doubloon' many characters interpret the signs on the gold coin nailed to the mast. All interpretations offer insight into the characters who gave them, but whose are to be chosen as the right ones? In a work as complex as *Moby Dick,* whose narrator is all too willing to insinuate that everything in the world has meaning, it is wise to be cautious about assigning a very specific or absolute meaning without assessing all possibilities.

Supernaturalism

A number of religious and superstitious viewpoints are offered the reader in *Moby Dick*. The Christian framework is qualified right from the start by Queequeg's reaction to it and by his own piety in worshipping Yojo. The pagan framework includes a great many characters, among whom are Stubb and Flask as well as the savages. The Parsee religion, here characterised by fire-worship and fatalism, is represented by Fedallah. Fatalism is a common belief of most of the characters in the work. Superstition is shared by Ahab, the Old Manx Sailor, and the crew. Certain sects of Christianity come in for satire—Bildad and Peleg have the rather laughable characteristics of some Quakers. Religious background, particularly Christian background, can seem sinister—in the cases, for example, of Ahab, who is a Quaker, and Gabriel, who is a Shaker. Questions of philosophical and religious kinds are constantly posed, but answers are not easy. Starbuck is a Quaker and Ishmael a Presbyterian; both seem to be primarily men of ideals and humanity. The frightening aspect of the supernatural in Moby Dick is that it involves everyone and every detail. The prophecies—of Elijah, of Gabriel, of Fedallah—come true. Ahab's conviction that he is possessed by some demonic spirit is in tune with his natural fatalism (his will is his fate). Ishmael is finally saved, but the reader cannot be certain that he deserves this any more than the other crew members, who all swore to follow Ahab to the death. The prophecy and the feeling of the necessity of the tragedy are related, as in Greek tragic drama. It is difficult to separate Ahab the man from the forces that may be driving him onward.

Characterisation

Ahab, Ishmael, and Starbuck

These are the three most rounded, or fully developed, characters in the book. Ahab, who has a family, is from the start bent on revenge against the whale, and his character is revealed to the reader gradually as he nears his prey. Since, in his first encounter with Moby Dick, he jumped at the whale with a knife, Ahab was certainly somewhat maniacal before he underwent the excruciating pain of losing his leg. He is keenly intelligent, a master over human nature, indomitably wilful, and ruthless in his quest. He does not think of his men, the ship owners, or his family in the final struggle, and there is no really cogent evidence that he ever has. Ishmael contrasts sharply with Ahab; he is opposite in nearly every respect. He is tolerant, jovial, naïve, frank, and content at sea. He likes to dream and to guess at the meanings of things. He respects religion. His humanity is revealed in his relationship with Queequeg; his detachment may be measured by how much he tells about his bunk-mate Bulkington, who is only a symbol, mentioned twice. Starbuck, unlike Ishmael, actually has the chance to change the course of events on the *Pequod*. But although he is intelligent, he lacks the willpower necessary to take decisive action outside his ordinary routine. Brave before whales, Starbuck quails before Ahab. He knows the cost of Ahab's quest and he is the only one who knows Ahab on a familiar basis. Yet he backs down from shooting Ahab, as he backed down from crossing him the first time Ahab announced that he was after Moby Dick. Like Ahab in having a family and in being an intelligent man, he is unlike him in force of will.

Other 'Knights and Squires'

Stubb is a pragmatist. He is good at his trade, but his final valuation of anything lies in its utility. He never questions Ahab's quest; he is good natured; he has a streak of sinister practical jesting in him—as when he asks Fleece to preach to the sharks. Flask is almost oblivious to everything around him. He asks no questions and is even unconcerned about the doubloon. Queequeg is known through Ishmael's close association with him. But more is learned about Ishmael than about Queequeg, for Queequeg moves in a world that is never described precisely, a world of fasting and meditation and Yojo and Kokovoko. He is a cannibal; he is the best harpooner in the book; he is prone to saving lives—he saves the captain of the *Moss,* Tashtego, and finally Ishmael. But he is like a natural force. He is unconscious, covered with ciphers he cannot understand. Daggoo and Tashtego are typical noble savages and professionally they are mere shadows to Queequeg.

Shipmates

The rest of the crew of the *Pequod* are minor characters at best. Fedallah, the Parsee, is an abstract representative of his sect (Chapters XLVIII, L, LXXIII, CXVII); he is a prophet but he has no sympathy for Ahab. The Old Manx Sailor (Chapters XL and CXXV) is the voice of sailors' superstitions. Bulkington is no more than a symbol of the ideal sailor (Chapters III and XXIII). The carpenter (Chapters CVII, CVIII, CXXVII) and Perth, the blacksmith (Chapters CXII-CXIII), are sounding-boards for Ahab, by which the reader can see the state of Ahab's damaged mind. Fleece, the ninety-year-old black cook

(Chapter LXIV), brings out the sinister aspects of Stubb and gives a sermon that rivals that of Father Mapple in its implications about the innate depravity of men. Pip, the cabin-boy, at first carefree, must face the hardship of labour and become mad (Chapters XL, XCIII, and CXXIX); like one of Shakespeare's fools or madmen, Pip often speaks better sense than Ahab, and the two are both called madmen by the Old Manx Sailor.

Shore people

Most of these characters are met in the way that accidental wanderings would allow. Peter Coffin, or 'Jonah', the landlord (Chapter II), is a practical joker. Father Mapple (Chapters VIII and IX) provides the keynote sermon for the whole book but is unknown as a man. Mrs Hosea Hussey (Chapters XV and XVII) is a satirical study of a hostess. Captains Peleg and Bildad (Chapters XVI, XVIII, XX, and XXII) are shrewd businessmen and devout hypocrites. Elijah (Chapters XIX and XXI) is a prophet only. Aunt Charity (Chapter XX; mentioned in Chapter LXXII) is a 'do-gooder'. Young Stiggs (Chapter XV), the nameless rigger (Chapter XXI), and unseen figures like the Squaw Tistig of Gayhead (Chapter XVI) are only mentioned.

Meetings at sea

The nine ships that the *Pequod* encounters in its journey each have their own character, and many of the figures are memorable minor sketches, such as the jovial Captain Boomer and the distraught Captain Gardiner. Most striking, however, are the chief characters in the anecdotes of Steelkilt and Radney (Chapter LIV) and of the Shaker Gabriel and Macey (Chapter LXXI). But in these cases character is subordinated to plot. Ishmael's friends on Tranque (Chapter CIII) and at Lima (Chapter LXXI) are very shadowy.

Part 4

Hints for study

First read *Moby Dick* through without external reference. Then, while the book is still fresh in your mind, write down your impressions of it in the form of sketches. If certain passages seem on retrospect to be outstanding for the light they shed on major themes in the work, seek them out and copy them word for word with a page reference for each. Try to summarise the action for yourself, and divide your summary into sections and even scenes. Where decisions are made by Ahab, Stubb or Starbuck, sum up what choices were involved. For example, Stubb's decision not to find redress for the kick administered by Ahab involves a resolve to have nothing further to do with Ahab and shows Stubb's inability—by temperament and by choice—to alter the course of events; another example is Starbuck's decision not to shoot Ahab with the musket. Now locate the action or actions which seem to be the major action or actions in the whole story, without which the work could not have taken place. Such actions in many cases are not in the work but precede it. For example, Ahab's previous encounter with Moby Dick, in which Ahab lost his leg, is a primary reason for Ahab's revenge.

With your notes as a support, you are now ready for a second reading, chapter by chapter, with this study guide and a dictionary. Two readings, *at least,* are essential if you are to discuss this work intelligently. During the second and subsequent readings you should consider the following points in addition to any ideas you have independently found interesting.

Points for detailed study

Themes

A theme is little more than a word, usually a general term or an abstraction, that requires interpretation or elaboration for understanding. Any literary work will deal with more than one theme, and in a good literary work the author will have taken great care to relate themes to one another. By writing about the way a single theme is used in a work, you will necessarily have to develop a theory of how that theme relates to other themes and to the significance or overall meaning of the work as a whole. A novel of the scope of *Moby Dick* will deal with many themes. The way the novel deals with any of these themes may provide you with the germ of a paper or a memorable reference for a test question. Consider the following themes as they are treated in the novel: *fate, obsession, madness, the sea, whaling, travel, experience, prophecy, work, communication, Quakers, genius, pragmatism, conflict, death, the castaway, Christianity*. Some, like *obsession, the sea,* and *whaling,* are more richly explored in this novel than others. Name three other themes in *Moby Dick* and list characters and actions you would use to discuss those themes.

Conflict

Conflict is what moves the story along and makes it full of suspense. *Moby Dick* has plenty of conflict. On a personal level Starbuck is in conflict with Ahab. On a natural level Ahab is in conflict with the whale. On a supernatural level Ahab is in conflict with the forces that drive him forward—himself, his fate, the dark powers with whom he says he is allied. The book contains anecdotes with their own conflicts—Gabriel and Macey or Steelkilt and Radney—but in each case these conflicts are related directly to Ahab's conflicts. Is not Ahab, like Gabriel, a fanatic who has unjustly taken over a ship for his own ends? All the conflict, however, is not confined to Ahab. Christianity and paganism are placed side by side for examination, as are capitalism and private motives, willpower and passivity, pragmatism and romanticism, innocence and experience, and so on. Can you name other examples of conflict in *Moby Dick?* Themes in conflict usually lead to some kind of resolution. How are conflicts resolved in this work, if at all?

Symbolism

A symbol is an object, a person, or an action that is very powerfully presented and usually emphasised by repetition or explicit commentary in the work. In some works many symbols are used. *Moby Dick* is a complex work with many symbols. The White Whale is perhaps the dominant symbol, but the doubloon that Ahab nails to the mast is also significant. Since Melville spent the whole book elaborating upon the meaning of Moby Dick and since he devoted a whole chapter to the sailors' interpretations of the doubloon, you can expect that the symbols in this work are not particularly easy to decipher. Who would have guessed, as Ahab finally did, that the second hearse to be seen on the sea—the one made of American wood—was to be the *Pequod?* Yet the very name *Pequod,* you are told, is that of a now extinct Indian tribe. Ahab, who seems to have a good eye for symbols, points out the irony of transforming a coffin into a lifebuoy, the symbol of death into the symbol of life. Ishmael points out another problem with symbols in his discussion of the whiteness of the whale. Traditional symbols with traditional meanings may be used thoughtlessly; white is a colour with traditional associations with innocence and purity, yet it has sinister overtones too. No dictionary of symbols will help you to discover the precise meanings of Melville's symbols. Their use in specific contexts is the only key to their meanings. Yojo is a symbol, not only for Queequeg but for the reader. The zodiacal signs inscribed on Queequeg's body are unintelligible to the savage, but indicate to us that Queequeg contains a mystical treatise on the heavens, which is transferred to the coffin that saves Ishmael. The sun is a symbol of goodness for Fedallah, but it is a symbol of evil for Ahab, even though he fixes the turned compass only by the position of the sun. Can you name other objects that have particular meanings for people in the book? Do they have another significance for you?

Look for associations with biblical figures to grasp the symbolical nature of characters. Both Ahab and Ishmael have evident association with biblical figures. How far does each association go? Melville is also fond of providing contrastive symbols. The White Whale seems conscious, purposive, malevolent towards man, and misshapen; in contrast the white squid seems unconscious, purposeless, oblivious of man, and formless. What can you do for the Right Whale and the Sperm Whale? Take Ishmael's own contrast of the two heads as a start. Not only colours, persons, beasts and objects, but also the weather, the heavenly bodies and human actions have special meanings in *Moby Dick*. Can you suggest a few contexts where the weather is significant for Ahab's quest? Are there places where the weather is symbolical of a mood opposite to the one suggested by the action?

Setting

An author's setting usually helps you to determine the meaning of a work. The setting includes the time, place, and circumstances in which the action occurs. In a great work of fiction, like *Moby Dick,* setting involves not only place but an attitude towards that place at a particular time in history. Besides the enormous and ever changing environment of the sea, Melville has included a number of land environments in New York, in New Bedford, and in Nantucket, and a number of vessels that the *Pequod* meets in its journey. In a time before the aeroplane, the sea was vast and travel on it slow. Whaling vessels were out for three or four years at a time. For Melville the sea represented life itself, with its profound depths and moody changes. The sea for men on the *Pequod* is a means of livelihood, a life's challenge, a friend, and an enemy. It is also the home of whales and particularly of Moby Dick. The vessels that sail on the sea each have their own characters; each represents a different interaction of captain and crew; each represents a different attitude towards Moby Dick and the whaling trade; each represents a different attitude towards life. The *Bachelor* is all gaiety; full of oil, she does not care for Moby Dick at all. The *Virgin* is empty of oil and of charity. The *Rachel* and the *Delight*, the *Town-Ho* and the *Jeroboam*, have met Moby Dick and faced disaster. Through the *Virgin*, the *Rose-Bud*, and the *Samuel Enderby* Melville makes fun of foreign whalers (all others being from Nantucket!). What nations are ridiculed? How? Can you discern any reason for the order in which the ships meet the *Pequod*? Can you compare or contrast the captains of any of these ships with Ahab?

Quotations for illustration

You will want to select from the novel certain quotations that you feel explain aspects of the work. The following are examples of the kinds of quotations you could select to illustrate the aspects indicated.

Character

Two quotations from Chapter XXVI will serve to show the flaw in Starbuck's character that inhibits him from confronting Ahab effectively:

> A staid, steadfast man, whose life for the most part was a telling pantomime of action, and not a tame chapter of sounds. Yet, for all his hardy sobriety and fortitude, there were certain qualities in him which at times affected, and in some cases seemed well nigh to overbalance all the rest. Uncommonly conscientious for a seaman, and endued with a deep natural reverence, the wild watery loneliness of his life did therefore strongly incline him to superstition, but to that sort of superstition, which in some organizations seems rather to spring, somehow, from intelligence than from ignorance.

> And brave as he might be, it was that sort of bravery chiefly, visible in some intrepid men, which, while generally abiding firm in the conflict with seas, or winds, or whales, or any of the ordinary irrational horrors of the world, yet cannot withstand those more terrific, because more spiritual terrors, which sometimes menace you from the concentrating brow of an enraged and mighty man.

Symbol

This quotation, from Chapter XLII, shows the profound significance of the White Whale's colour:

> But not yet have we solved the incantation of this whiteness, and learned why it appeals with such power to the soul; and more strange and far more portentous—why, as we have seen, it is at once the most meaning symbol of spiritual things, nay, the very veil of the Christian's Deity; and yet should be as it is, the intensifying agent in things the most appalling to mankind.

Theme

Ahab's obsession is clearly seen in his many soliloquies, in which he speaks aloud, as if to himself, his innermost torments. Chapter CXXXV provides such a soliloquy, just before Ahab's final struggle with Moby Dick:

> 'What a lovely day again! were it a new-made world, and made for a summer-house to the angels, and this morning the first of its throwing open to them, a fairer day could not dawn upon that world. Here's food for thought, had Ahab time to think; but Ahab never thinks; he only feels, feels, feels; *that's* tingling enough for mortal man! to think's audacity. God only has that right and privilege. Thinking is, or ought to be, a coolness and a calmness; and our poor hearts throb, and our poor brains beat too much for that . . . Were I the wind, I'd blow no more on such a wicked, miserable world. I'd crawl somewhere to a cave, and slink there.'

Ishmael and Queequeg

This complex relationship, involving themes such as brotherhood, savagery, tolerance, religion and endurance, grows gradually in the book, but Ishmael's sympathy for the savage begins clearly in Chapter X, when Ishmael watches Queequeg 'read':

> With much interest I sat watching him. Savage though he was, and hideously marred about the face—at least to my taste—his countenance yet had something in it which was by no means disagreeable. You cannot hide the soul. Through all his unearthly tatooings, I thought I saw the traces of a simple honest heart; and in his large, deep eyes, fiery black and bold, there seemed tokens of a spirit that would dare a thousand devils.

Fedallah and Ahab

Although Ahab deserts Fedallah for Pip late in the book, he believes superstitiously in Fedallah's prophecies, and for good reason: they all come true. The theme of fate, prophecy, dreams, demonic power, the sun, and pride are involved in this relationship. On the ocean for the night, Ahab in Chapter CXVII awakens after a horrifying dream about hearses, and Fedallah comforts him as follows:

'But I said, old man, that ere thou couldst die on this voyage, two hearses must verily be seen by thee on the sea; the first not made by mortal hands; and the visible wood of the last one must be grown in America . . . I shall still go before thee thy pilot . . . Hemp only can kill thee.'

Ahab himself recognises the second hearse before the reader does in Chapter CXXXV, after Fedallah has perished and after the first hearse has been seen:

'The ship! The hearse!—the second hearse!' cried Ahab from the boat; 'its wood could only be American!'
   Diving beneath the settling ship, the whale ran quivering along its keel; but turning under water, swiftly shot to the surface again, far off the other bow, but within a few yards of Ahab's boat, where, for a time, he lay quiescent.

Ishmael's mentality

Ishmael has a symbol-seeking mind. He is on a lifelong quest for meaning, analogous to Ahab's quest for *Moby Dick,* and in a way both Ishmael and Ahab are very close to, but can never actually obtain, the things they seek. Ishmael's thoughts on Bulkington in Chapter XXIII show how a character becomes a symbol for an idea in Ishmael's mind and how Ishmael challenges the reader to grapple with what the character means:

Know ye, now, Bulkington? Glimpses do ye seem to see of that mortally intolerable truth; that all deep, earnest thinking is but the intrepid effort of the soul to keep the open independence of her sea; while the wildest winds of heaven and earth conspire to cast her on the treacherous, slavish shore?

Notice here how the antithesis, or opposition, of land and sea is used to denote spiritual states of man. Thought itself is heroic, like a voyage on open seas. The universe seems to be opposed to free thought, hurling the thinker back on land, where the mind is forever enslaved.

Ahab's humanity

Although pictured as mad, Ahab has the fears and longings of other men; only when those emotions seem to be very strong, his indomitable will turns him back to his mad quest. One purpose of the character Starbuck is to bring out the humanity of Ahab. Another is to show that Ahab is beyond humanity's efforts to reclaim. In Chapter CXXXII Ahab's tear is a sign of a humanity that he must wilfully abandon:

Slowly crossing the deck from the scuttle, Ahab leaned over the side, and watched how his shadow in the water sank and sank to his gaze, the more and the more that he strove to ' pierce the profundity . . . That glad, happy air, that winsome sky, did at last stroke and caress him; the step-mother world, so long cruel—forbidding—now threw affectionate arms round his stubborn neck, and did seem to joyously sob over him, as if over one, that however wilful and erring, she could yet find it in her heart to save and to bless. From beneath his slouched hat Ahab dropped a tear into the sea; nor did all the Pacific contain such wealth as that one wee drop.

The world is personified as a caring, forgiving step-mother to the orphaned Ahab. Nature seems to have the power to restore men to themselves. Yet Ahab in the ensuing conversation with Starbuck cannot turn away from his plan.

Jest and earnest

Moby Dick is full of humour, but nearly every jest has serious meaning behind it. For example, the sermon that Fleece is made to give to the sharks in Chapter LXIV provides a humorous parody of Father Mapple's sermon in Chapter IX. The situation itself is absurd. How can sharks understand man's speech? Even Fleece's manner of expression—the candid attempt to moralise, the black dialect, the sermonic techniques—is meant to inspire laughter. Yet the message is all too clear and serious—men are like sharks, vicious and self-centred and unheeding:

'Your woraciousness, fellow-critters, I don't blame ye so much for; dat is natur, and can't be helped; but to gobern dat wicked natur, dat is de pint. You is sharks, sartin; but if you gobern de shark in you, why den you be angel; for all angel is not'ing more dan de shark well goberned.'

According to Fleece men are all depraved; goodness is only a result of an evil man's heroic attempt to overcome the limitations of his condition. Even worse, Fleece says that Stubb is more sinister than a shark: 'I'm bressed if he ain't more of shark dan Massa Shark hisself.'

Social satire

The nineteenth century was an age of self-righteousness. As with today, many of the institutions purportedly designed to alleviate misery or better the condition of mankind were products not of humanitarians but of hypocrites who foisted their own beliefs off on others as a means of exerting their power. In Chapter LXV Ishmael lashes out against those who, while against cannibalism, actually indulge in worse crimes themselves:

> Cannibals? who is not a cannibal? I tell you it will be more tolerable for the Fejee that salted down a lean missionary in his cellar against a coming famine; it will be more tolerable for that provident Fejee, I say, in the day of judgment, than for thee, civilized and enlightened gourmand, who nailest geese to the ground and feastest on their bloated livers in thy paté-de-foie-gras.

Arrangement of material

A quotation will not stand in its own defence. You should explain precisely why you use them. In preparing for writing a paper or examination, you should frame likely questions to answer and then answer them with as much detail as you can. You will have to refer to events and characters with economy and accuracy, giving only enough information to refresh in your readers' minds the salient portions of the novel. In answering a question be sure to limit yourself to that specific consideration. Do not get sidetracked or give so many examples that your readers tire of your argument.

Your answer should begin with a strong statement of your own point of view. You should set the limits of your answer and, where possible, enumerate your points. Then develop each point with specific reference to the novel. It is always difficult to judge exactly how much detail is necessary to prove your point, but too much is always preferable to too little. Do not equivocate in your answer. A strong answer with a few details wrong is better than a weak answer with no controlling force for the correct details.

There follow some questions you might pose for yourself about *Moby Dick*.

(1) Does Ahab become progressively mad in the course of *Moby Dick* or does he begin mad and remain mad throughout?

(2) What is Ishmael's attitude towards the story he relates?

(3) How is Father Mapple's two-part sermon about Jonah in Chapter IX relevant to the story about Ahab and Ishmael?

(4) Why does Ishmael spend fully one-third of the novel telling about whales and whaling when the main story seems to be that of Captain Ahab?

(5) The *Pequod* meets nine other ships in its journey to the Japanese Cruising Grounds *(Goney, Town-Ho, Jeroboam, Jungfrau, Rose-Bud, Samuel Enderby, Bachelor, Rachel* and *Delight)*. Choosing any three, compare or contrast them with the *Pequod*.

(6) What is the relationship and what is the conflict between Starbuck and Ahab?

(7) Prophecy, dreams, and portents abound in the book, and many of them seem to be true. What attitude or attitudes towards fate and predestination do you discern in the work?

(8) The harpooners Queequeg, Daggoo, and Tashtego are all types of noble savages. Characterise their attitudes towards the events they encounter.

(9) Explore the symbolism of the doubloon that is to be the reward for sighting Moby Dick. Does the doubloon have one explicit meaning? If so, give it. If not, say why not.

(10) Fedallah and Ahab have opposite attitudes towards the sun and fire. What is the basis for their beliefs and why do they disagree?

(11) Stubb forces the ninety-year-old cook, Fleece, to lecture to the sharks about charity. What is the irony in the sermon? How does this sermon compare with the one Father Mapple gave in Chapter IX? (Use the quotation cited above as an aid.)

(12) Queequeg left Kokovoko, his native island, to discover in Christendom a better way of living. What did he conclude about the value of Christian living, as it is practised in the 'civilised' world? What are the implications of this view in *Moby Dick* as a whole?

(13) Choosing *either* the anecdote about Steelkilt and Radney *or* the anecdote about the Shaker Gabriel and Macey, explore the relation of anecdote to Ahab's story in detail.

(14) Queequeg and Ishmael have a very close relationship for the majority of the book. Trace this relationship from their first meeting to the final salvation of Ishmael by Queequeg's coffin-turned-lifebuoy to show the kinds of bonds that unite them.

(15) Humour abounds in *Moby Dick*. What is the purpose of humour in the book when the story of Ahab is really a tragedy?

(16) *Moby Dick,* while a novel, has been classified as an epic, a tragedy, a comedy, and an anatomy (a kind of encyclopedia of information about a particular human endeavour). Classify the novel as one of these four types and defend your classification.

(17) Ahab is the most intelligent man on the *Pequod;* in fact, he is a genius. Defend or refute this idea.

(18) What is Pip's function with relation to Ahab? to Ishmael?

(19) Although *Moby Dick* is a sea story, it contains many comments upon life ashore. What does the shore represent for Ishmael? How does satire complement Ishmael's view of the shore?

(20) Point of view in *Moby Dick* is not consistent. Ishmael is clearly the narrator for most of the work, but often stage directions imply that the book becomes a play at times; elsewhere other figures (Pip, Fleece, Fedallah, and Stubb, for example) are allowed to comment directly on the action. Why should Melville have preferred to use many points of view with which to elaborate his story?

(21) The Great Squid and the White Whale are contrastive symbols, much like the Right Whale head and the Sperm Whale head. Choose one or the other of these pairs of contrastive symbols and explore their meanings.

(22) Ishmael always seeks meaning. Does he ever learn anything in *Moby Dick*?

(23) Discuss one of the following themes as it is woven through the book: *isolation, endurance, feelings, temperance, history, infinity.*

(24) What do the allusions to natural history, history, literature, and the arts do for your understanding of Ahab's quest of the whale? Put another way, why did Melville not rest satisfied with giving his readers *only* the action involving Ahab and the whale?

(25) The tragedy of *Moby Dick* is as much the tragedy of man as it is the tragedy of Ahab. Using Ahab's interaction with his crew as a start, elaborate upon this idea.

Model answers

The answers provided for the following four questions are intended to be models only, not absolute and definitive answers. The method of answering is more important than the content of the answers.

---

(1) *Does Ahab become progressively mad in the course of* Moby Dick *or does he begin mad and remain mad throughout?*

Ahab's 'madness' is his obsession to seek revenge against the White Whale at all costs. Ironically the very qualities that make him heroic— his intensity, determination, strength of will, and sense of purpose— also make him flawed. The seeds of Ahab's madness are in his essential character. He is maniacal when he first attacks Moby Dick with only a knife, and his desperate thrust of the harpoon at the end of the book is like the first attack in its irrationality. Yet Ahab's madness is carefully concealed from his crew and from Captains Bildad and Peleg, and the reader is only gradually made aware of Ahab's tragical state of mind.

Ishmael is apprehensive about Ahab after he first signs on the *Pequod,* and the assurances of Captain Peleg do not convince him that 'Ahab has his humanities'. In fact, all evidence points to the unusual character of Ahab. When the prophet Elijah warns Ishmael about the impending voyage, he compounds Ishmael's fears about the man named for the tragical biblical king, whose blood dogs licked. Ahab's reclusiveness, no less than dockside superstitions, adds to the impression that Ahab is unusual.

Ahab does not appear on deck until late in the voyage. Soon afterwards his colloquy with the crew is the first sign that he has other designs than to fill the hold with whale oil. The crew are magnetised by his willpower, and they agree to follow and kill Moby Dick—all but Starbuck. Ahab's foreknowledge of his crew's reaction shows how deeply he has thought about his revenge and how certain he is that he can manipulate men's minds.

Throughout the voyage Ahab's desire to kill the White Whale is emphasised. Every ship's captain is asked about the whale. The discovery of the special boat crew with Fedallah and the Philippino crew, the forging of a special harpoon to kill the whale, the sleepless watches of Fedallah and Ahab, the concern for all portents and signs of good or evil, and the special basket for Ahab's final sightings of Moby Dick, indicate an intelligent—inhumanly intelligent—programme. Ahab's intellectual prowess extends to his fixing the turned compass; his intuition enables him to find Moby Dick. Nearly all Ahab's decisions are based on his quest for the whale. Even when he delays to kill some other whale or empty the hold to repair a leak, Ahab is interested in keeping his crew busy or happy, not in delaying for its own sake.

In the final days of the pursuit Ahab's soliloquies show him to be suffering not only from lack of sleep but also from mental pangs. He dreams of killing the whale; he dreams of hearses. Ahab becomes more nervous about every sign than he has been before. As he nears the whale, his whole being is devoted to the hunt. He associates himself with Pip, the mad cabin-boy, and he openly acknowledges his own madness.

Ironically, in his final hours Ahab comes the closest to admitting his own humanity. Starbuck notices that Ahab sheds a tear—a sign of humanity. Yet Starbuck cannot even then dissuade Ahab from his quest. It is not clear that Ahab has the slightest inkling that the *Pequod,* like him, is doomed. Yet he is responsible for the *Pequod's* destruction. His final farewell to the sea and to Starbuck indicate his presentiment of his death. His final thrust with the harpoon is done in despair. But the hempen kink that pulls him to his death is accidental, unexpected, and sudden.

Ahab is most eloquent when his concentration on his quest is most complete. Magnificent, even in torment, master over the elements, a natural leader of men, Ahab's passion, not his intellect, triumphs in the end. As he admits, feelings, not thoughts, are his governing agencies. Surrendering to his passionate will, his death is inevitable, even necessary. Defined by his quest rather than his humanity, he is more an elegant machine than a man. His obsession makes him mad.

---

(5) *The* Pequod *meets nine other ships in its journey to the Japanese Cruising Grounds. Choosing any three, compare or contrast them with the* Pequod.

The nine ships that the *Pequod* passes on its journey are representative of the range of possibilities in the whaling business. Ships can be very successful, as is the *Bachelor*, or unsuccessful, as is the *Jungfrau*; they can be victims of struggles among crews and mates as with the *Town-Ho* and *Jeroboam*, or they can be victims of incompetent captains, as with the *Rose-Bud*. But just as each of the nine ships relates to the whaling trade, so each relates to life itself. The nine ships and the *Pequod* must sail on the sea of life and kill whales and, perhaps, meet Moby Dick. The last three ships encountered by the *Pequod* provide interesting comparisons and contrasts with her, particularly with regard to their encounters (or lack of encounters) with Moby Dick.

After seeing three ships from Nantucket (*Goney, Town-Ho* and *Jeroboam*) with mystery in their encounters with Moby Dick, and three foreign ships (*Jungfrau, Rose-Bud,* and *Samuel Enderby*), which are satirised as incompetent, the *Pequod* encounters three more Nantucket ships (*Bachelor, Rachel* and *Delight*), which serve as warnings of a ship's fate when she decides to seek Moby Dick as prey. The *Bachelor* is so full of oil that it is stored everywhere. Members of the crew and native girls dance on her decks and all the flags are out to show how cheery the ship is. The *Bachelor* has not seen Moby Dick and does not wish ever to see that hated whale. She seems to serve as a model for monetary prosperity—but only when Moby Dick is not even contemplated. The *Pequod* perhaps has the expertise to end her voyage like the *Bachelor*, but clearly Ahab could never be released from his quest. He spurns the convivial captain's invitation to a gam.

The *Rachel* has lost a boat to Moby Dick. Captain Gardiner reports that his young son was last seen in a boat pulled away by Moby Dick, to which he was attached. Gardiner tries to persuade Ahab to help in the search for his son, but Ahab sends him away. The loss of a son of a fellow-Nantucketer cannot lure Ahab from his quest, even though he may be accused of uncharitability. Just as Ahab gives no thought to his wife and family in his quest, so here he does not value Gardiner's loss. The *Rachel* continues to look for its lost whaleboat—and lucky it is for Ishmael, who is picked up by her.

The *Delight* has on her deck an emblem of the destruction of Moby Dick. A whaleboat stove in by the White Whale is an emblem of Ahab's own destruction, but Ahab scorns the statement by the captain of the *Delight* that no harpoon can kill the White Whale. The *Delight* is aptly named not for the loss of the whaleboat but for the grace that no man died besides the crew of the whaleboat in struggling with the whale.

So the *Bachelor* is a sign to the *Pequod* of the success of normal whaling. The *Rachel* is a portent of the loss that may be the *Pequod's* too. The *Delight* is a much more urgent warning that some full tragedy awaits him who hunts the whale. In fact Ahab himself averts his eyes when the *Delight* buries the dead man; a voice from astern cries out at the portentous coffin tied to the *Pequod's* stern.

---

(14) *Queequeg and Ishmael have a very close relationship for the majority of the book. Trace this relationship from their first meeting to the final salvation of Ishmael by Queequeg's coffin-turned-lifebuoy to show the kinds of bonds that unite them.*

Queequeg and Ishmael are thrown together quite by accident, yet they become bound by a friendship that cuts across lines of race, religion, and background. At first Ishmael's prejudices have the upper hand. His mysterious bed-mate at the Spouter-Inn turns out to be a tattooed cannibal who flies into bed with a tomahawk in his teeth. Queequeg's habits—of dressing, of worship, and of eating—amuse Ishmael, but Ishmael finally decides that Queequeg is a kind man.

Queequeg says that Ishmael and he are married. The two share pipes, stories, and a wheelbarrow, and decide to ship aboard the whaler *Pequod* together. Although they are opposite in some respects—their whaling experience, thought processes, and heroic stature—the two are bound on the *Pequod* by the monkey-rope, in a whaleboat in the centre of the whales' breeding-ground, and through the coffin-turned-lifebuoy. Their brotherhood is untrammelled by Ishmael's attempts to convert his friend to Christianity; indeed, Ishmael engages in Yojo-worship for the sake of fellowship, just as Queequeg goes to hear Father Mapple. Queequeg represents the heroic, masculine virtues to the end—he saves the captain of the *Moss*, Tashtego, and, through his coffin, Ishmael. Ishmael represents the contemplative feminine virtues—he even ends up a castaway like Pip, and perhaps his state of mind in telling the story is a product of his isolation in the centre of the vast ocean.

The reason for these figures' close bond involves their naïvety. Queequeg has written on his skin a treatise on the heavens, but he understands no more of this than of the book that he used in the Spouter-Inn. Ishmael attempts candidly to interpret everything, using every resource available—historical, literary, fantastical—yet in the end he is little more educated than at the beginning. Queequeg, like the other savages, is unconcerned by the turn of events and oblivious of any personal danger. Ishmael is very conscious of what is going on around him. Yet their ends are integrally related. If Queequeg decides to die from his ague, the coffin will be used for his burial. Since he does not, the coffin is caulked to become the lifebuoy for Ishmael. The reward of the buoy is not planned by Ishmael, but a matter of fate. Again, intellect can take Ishmael so far and no further. As extremes, then, Ishmael's contemplative, conscious state of mind and Queequeg's intuitive, unconscious state of mind are complementary. Both finally rely on fate, and the unconscious, not the conscious, can provide the saving actions.

---

(21) *The Great Squid and the White Whale are contrastive symbols, much like the Right Whale head and the Sperm Whale head. Choose one or the other of these pairs of contrastive symbols and explore their meanings.*

The Great Squid and the White Whale are contrastive symbols. Although it would be dangerous to assign absolute meanings to either, they provide enough points of contrast to indicate that each is a universal force as well as a sea beast, and that each is related to the other. The size, colour, and environment of these creatures are similar. They are enormous; they are white; they inhabit the most profound ocean. The squid is the supposed food of the sperm whale; yet the white squid would be too large for the White Whale to eat.

The major point of contrast is in the creatures' shapes. Even though the whale is said to be indescribable by man, it is easily the more clearly defined of the two beasts. The squid is almost wholly shapeless. It is a mass of white with anaconda arms, teeming below the surface. It seems to be a white blob. On the other hand the White Whale has a form that is fish-like, even though no man can aptly draw it. It has a head, eyes, teeth, bones and so forth.

The problem with shape has a complementary problem in the purposiveness of these creatures. The Great Squid seems aimless and purposeless. It is passive, meant to be eaten. It seems some amorphous principle. The White Whale, on the other hand, has at least the purpose of killing its pursuers. It also saves other harpooned whales. In fact, it seems to be conscious and determined to wreak destruction. Here it is wholly opposite to the Great Squid.

If the two are to be assigned meanings, the Great Squid may be the formless chaos out of which the purposive natural forces take their nourishment; it may be potentiality; it may be the amoeba-like passive nature envisioned by the Romantic poets as benign, formless, supporting or informing form. The White Whale, with which the lookouts confuse the Great Squid, would then be the purposive natural force; it may be activity availing itself of its tremendous powers; it may be the actively destructive god in a world of sinister battles between good and evil forces, where the forces of good are largely passive and destructible.

Part 5

Suggestions for further reading

Editions of the text of *Moby Dick*

HAYFORD, HARRISON, HERSCHEL PARKER, AND G. THOMAS TANSELLE (eds.), Evanston and Chicago, Northwest University Press and the Newberry Library, Illinois, 1968. The Northwestern-Newberry Edition. This is intended to be the standard text of *Moby Dick*. It supersedes the former standard edition: Luther Mansfield and Howard Vincent, eds. Hendricks House, New York, 1952.

HAYFORD, HARRISON AND HERSCHEL PARKER (eds.), W. W. Norton, New York, 1967. The Norton Critical Edition. This includes the text, reviews and letters by Melville, analogues and sources, and excerpts from selected criticisms. Illustrations of whaling and an extensive glossary of nautical terms makes this a useful edition.

FEIDELSON, CHARLES JR. (ed.), Bobbs-Merrill, Indianapolis, Indiana, 1964. The Library of Literature Edition. This is an excellent classroom text with illustrations of whaling, a thoughtful introduction, and extensive critical notes at the bottom of the page.

Two other editions, aimed at the general reader are:

BEAVER, HAROLD, (ed.), Penguin Books, Harmonsworth, 1975.

KAZIN, ALFRED, (ed.), the Riverside Edition, Houghton Mifflin, Boston, 1956.

Other works by Melville

The standard edition for all Melville's writings is the Northwestern-Newberry Edition (see above).

Bibliographies of Melville's works

BLANCK, JACOB, *Bibliography of American Literature*, Yale University Press, New Haven, Connecticut, 1955-   , Vol. 6, 1973.

TANSELLE, G. THOMAS, *A Checklist of Editions of Moby-Dick, 1851-1976*, Northwestern University Press and the Newberry Library, Evanston and Chicago, Illinois, 1976.

Books about Melville

HOWARD, LEON, *Herman Melville: A Biography,* University of California Press, Berkeley, 1951; reprinted 1958. The standard life.

LEYDA, JAY, *The Melville Log: A Documentary Life of Herman Melville 1819-1891.* Two vols., Harcourt Brace, New York, 1951, reprinted Gordion Press, New York, 1969. The major work of Melville scholarship.

MILLER, EDWIN HAVILAND, *Melville,* George Braziller, New York, 1975.

SEALTS, MERTON M., JR., *The Early Lives of Melville: Nineteenth-Century Biographical Sketches and Their Authors,* University of Wisconsin Press, Madison, Wisconsin, 1974.

Criticism

BAIRD, JAMES, *Ishmael,* Johns Hopkins University Press, Baltimore, 1956.

BERTHOFF, WARNER, *The Example of Melville,* Princeton University Press, Princeton, 1962. An outstanding introduction to Melville's work.

BOWEN, MARTIN, *The Long Encounter: Self and Experience in the Writings of Herman Melville,* University of Chicago Press, Chicago, 1960.

OLSON, CHARLES, *Call Me Ishmael,* Reynall and Hitchcock, New York, 1947, reprinted Grove Press, New York, 1958.

STERN, MILTON R., *The Fine-Hammered Steel of Herman Melville,* University of Illinois Press, Urbana, 1957.

THOMPSON, LAWRENCE R., *Melville's Quarrel with God,* Princeton University Press, Princeton, 1952.

Collections of critical essays

BOWEN, JAMES K. AND RICHARD VAN DER BEETS, *A Critical Guide to Herman Melville: Abstracts of Forty Years of Criticism.* Scott Foresman, Glenview, Illinois, 1971.

GILMORE, MICHAEL T. (ed.), *Twentieth-Century Interpretations of Moby Dick,* Prentice-Hall, Englewood Cliffs, New Jersey, 1971. Contains an introductory essay, ten good interpretive essays, and twelve excerpts from other criticisms.

PARKER, HERSCHEL, AND HARRISON HAYFORD, (eds.), *Moby Dick as Doubloon: Essays and Extracts (1851-1970),* W. W. Norton, New York, 1970. An outstanding casebook intended as a companion to the Norton Critical Edition of *Moby Dick,* listed above, this contains seventy-one reviews of the novel, 1851-2, fifty-six critical extracts, 1853-1925, seventy-four critical extracts, 1926-70, and an annotated, chronological bibliography of books and articles, 1921-69.

VINCENT, HOWARD P. (ed.), *Charles E. Merrill Studies in Moby Dick,* Charles E. Merrill, Columbus, Ohio, 1969. Contains five reviews and eighteen excerpts.

ZOLLNER, ROBERT, *The Salt-Sea Mastodon: A Modern Reading of Moby Dick,* University of California Press, Berkeley and Los Angeles, 1973.

The author of these notes

WILSON F. ENGEL is a graduate of the University of Wisconsin—Madison (Ph.D.); he has held teaching posts at the University of Wisconsin at Richland and at the University of Edinburgh (1976-7) and is now an Assistant Professor at Allentown College, Center Valley, Pennsylvania. He has written various articles and his edition of James Shirley's *The Gentlemen of Venice* was published in 1976. He is also the author of the York Notes *Quentin Durward*.

The first ten titles

YORK HANDBOOKS form a companion series to York Notes and are designed to meet the wider needs of students of English and related fields. Each volume is a compact study of a given subject area, written by an authority with experience in communicating the essential ideas to students of all levels.

AN INTRODUCTORY GUIDE TO ENGLISH LITERATURE
by MARTIN STEPHEN

PREPARING FOR EXAMINATIONS IN ENGLISH LITERATURE
by NEIL McEWAN

AN INTRODUCTION TO LITERARY CRITICISM
by RICHARD DUTTON

THE ENGLISH NOVEL
by IAN MILLIGAN

ENGLISH POETRY
by CLIVE T. PROBYN

STUDYING CHAUCER
by ELISABETH BREWER

STUDYING SHAKESPEARE
by MARTIN STEPHEN *and* PHILIP FRANKS

ENGLISH USAGE
by COLIN G. HEY

A DICTIONARY OF LITERARY TERMS
by MARTIN GRAY

READING THE SCREEN
An Introduction to Film Studies
by JOHN IZOD